MW01109038

Lt. Herschel D. Ponder

to understand. I am now beginning
to see what a mean and treacherous
thing this war is. Tell you more about
it someday.

So, Si, glad to meet Marjorie, but there's

> I am now beginning to see what a mean
> and treacherous thing this war is.
> Tell you more about it someday.
>
> 25 October 1944

and thought and no May — did I know.
I was wondering if I should. Then I
got another letter and now I know
who Marjorie is. "Hi Margie, hear
you went to the "Hill." More good
people go to that place than anyplace
I ever saw. Some of them have blue
eyes and dark hair and are very
pretty. Don't you think so. On second
thought — I'm telling you, not asking.
You know, Margie, I sure do envy you.
Why? Cause, you're where I want to be

THIS WWII WARRIOR brought to life the riveting story of one of many heroes and his deeds. His, however, contains a very important added dimension — that of highlighting the added tragedy of Post Traumatic Stress Disorder or PTSD. His experience clearly profoundly impacted his quality of life, much like that suffered by many veterans of our recent wars in Iraq and Afghanistan. His personal story must be read and told over and over today — to honor him and his sacrifice in a way that can help so many of our Veterans and their family members.

Lieutenant General Hubert G. Smith, U. S. Army. Retired

WATCHING THE PRESENTATION of *Ponder Anew* and having read the entire memoir — as a former Airman in the USAF, then as a Chaplain in both The USAF and The US Army, and now as a Mental Health professional working with Warriors from Iraq and Afghanistan — I was brought to tears as I was forced to relive the sights, sounds and smells of combat. This is a must-see and must-read for every former or current Service member and their family members — if we ever hope to appreciate what we and our loved ones have experienced in "The Fog of War."

Frank M. Brannon: Licensed Professional Counselor,
Mental Health Service Provider

Ponder Anew

What the Almighty Can Do

A WWII Warrior's Story

Herschel D. Ponder

PUBLISHED BY WESTVIEW, INC.
KINGSTON SPRINGS, TENNESSEE

PUBLISHED BY WESTVIEW, INC.
P.O. Box 605
Kingston Springs, TN 37082
www.publishedbywestview.com

ISBN 978-1-937763-92-3

First edition, May 2013

Printed in the United States of America on acid free paper.

Acknowledgements

We would like to thank the following people for their kind and essential support in bringing Lt. Herschel D. Ponder's war memories to print:

Schell Ponder Alexander
Rev. Battle Alexander Beasley
Eric Booth
Frank M. Brannon
Anne Ponder Brookhouse
Janie Chaffin
John Chaffin
Chaffin's Barn Dinner Theater
Brigadier General Frank Cunningham, III, US Army, Ret.
Dugger Mountain Music Hall
Walter C. Gray, III
Howard Davis Grier
Amy Dawn Harwell
The Hermitage Artist Retreat
Colonel Ralph C. Jenkins, US Army Air Corps, Ret.
Mildred Kiefer
Richard Kiefer
Summerfield Q. Mobley, DVM
Charles D. Mohrle
David Morris
Mary Catharine Nelson
Potts Marketing Group, LLC, especially Tom Potts and
    Greg Potts
Jim Reyland and Audio Productions
Lieutenant General Hubert G. Smith, US Army, Ret.
Tennessee Women's Theater Project
Bob Welch, Education Director, Frontiers of Flight
    Museum, Dallas, TX

Table of Contents

Acknowledgements vii

Preface by Carol Ponder xi

Foreword to the 2013 Edition xvii

SEPTEMBER 22, 1942. 1

CAPT. B. E. KIESLER 2

MIAMI BEACH 12

SAAC CENTER 31

CIMMARON FIELD — OKLAHOMA CITY 35

THE FLIGHT LINE 39

BASIC TRAINING — ENID, OKLAHOMA 46

ADVANCED FLYING TRAINING 52

RICHMOND ARMY AIR FORCE BASE 65

NORFOLK, VIRGINIA 71

OVERSEAS 80

SHREWSBURY 83

ASSIGNMENT TO A COMBAT UNIT 85

405th GROUP — 510th FIGHTER SQUADRON 88

COL. RALPH JENKINS 90

MY FIRST MISSION 91

WARREN GLENN TRANTHAM 102

THE FIVE OF US! 105

SUSPECTED SABOTAGE 121

TREE BLASTS 123

THE COUNTER ATTACK 133

DOC MILLIGAN 143

ZWARTBERG, BELGIUM Y-32 155

CHESTER A. BLACK 170

HOWARD I. "HI" PRICE 189

MAJ. HARRY SANDERS, OPERATIONS OFFICER ..216

OCTOBER 29, 1945 — FORT BRAGG, NORTH
CAROLINA 257

About Carol Ponder and Robert Kiefer 285

Preface by Carol Ponder

My father, Herschel Doyle Ponder (Herschel), was a complicated man. An only child, he was born and raised in the Appalachian Mountains around Asheville, North Carolina to a huge extended family that had lived there since the late 1700s. Education, the arts, politics, community, and church were all important to that family: My father grew up painting with oils, acting on stage, and singing in choirs as well as going to school, playing basketball and tennis, and hunting and fishing. His mother taught first grade at Valley Springs public school and his father worked for Southern Railway (after realizing he couldn't adequately support his family on two teachers' salaries, a decision my father emulated later in his own life). It was to defend this rich life, and for love of the country where it was possible, that my father enlisted in the Army Air Corp on September 22, 1942.

My mother, Mary Eleanor Israel (Eleanor), and her brother, James O. Israel, Jr. (Jim) also were born and raised to a large Mountain family for whom education, the arts, politics, community, and church were integral parts of life. (The order of importance, as in my father's family, depended on with whom you spoke.) She described my father to me as "...very carefully raised." Mom recognized his tremendous capacity for empathy and compassion soon after they met; it was part of what drew her to him. They met just before he went overseas to fly P-47 Thunderbolts over the European theater in WWII and courted through letters during the war. My father survived the war; but, in part because of his capacity for compassion, he was profoundly changed by his experiences in it. Still, love survived and they were married on June 22, 1946. They had three children — my two sisters and me — and it was for us that Dad wrote his WWII memoir in 1989, 44 years after his war ended.

When I read the memoir for the first time, I had a sense that he wanted me to understand why he was as he was. Today we speak of the "visible and invisible" wounds of war, and I believe that's what he was trying to address. His thyroid almost completely ceased functioning by the end of his war — something his doctors could never explain and which it took them months to diagnose — but this hardly accounts for all with which he struggled. He had a mercurial temperament. Growing up, I knew that sometimes he could be angrier than I might expect in one minute and gently kind in the next. I learned that he suffered from fierce headaches, as well as stomach problems, and that there were times when I just needed to be quiet because he was resting. Sometimes he seemed to be (what I now recognize as) depressed; other times, he disappeared into the basement family room where he listened to the music of Bach and Beethoven, Mozart and Wagner, sometimes silently weeping in joy, sometimes calling me downstairs to share the music with him. He was capable of incredible physical energy and vitality, yet sometimes would collapse in exhaustion after an ordinary day. He often expressed wonderful generosity with family, friends, and community — yet also reflected, not infrequently, that the world somehow owed him more, that he never quite received what he deserved for what he had given up.

Until I was grown, I never heard my father talk much about WWII. I remember that, in my mid-40s, Mom told me that he suffered from nightmares for many years after the war and was sometimes withdrawn. From Dad's memoir, I finally learned about his war and the deep joys, sorrows, horrors, and delights of his experiences in it. In his writing, he didn't pull any punches. He wrote as he remembered. He treated both his "bad" and "good" actions and experiences evenly, neither prettying things up nor downplaying his own skills as a pilot and survivor. He wrote about the war's winding down, the sudden cessation of action, coming home, and finding himself a stranger in his own land where he was, "...working like hell to keep my insides from jumping through my skin." Through all of it, Dad wrote with his ever-present sense of humor, a soldier's — and highlander's — exquisite appreciation of irony.

In preparing Herschel Ponder's memoir for publication, I have honored his process as a storyteller. Dad sat at a table, writing in longhand on long, yellow legal pads. Although the memoir is roughly chronological, he told the story as he remembered it — with side trips into personalities, places, experiences, events, and scenery as he felt necessary to the telling. To preserve his voice, I have preserved much of his idiosyncratic punctuation: Dad used dashes — a lot. Every time I browse in the memoir, I hear his voice — the dashes and other punctuation represent phrasing and pauses for dramatic effect or to emphasize meaning, as if he were telling the story out loud. My editorial changes are sparse, comprising a few punctuation alterations and spelling or word substitution where, in my judgment, the original transcriptionist may have misread his handwriting, especially of an idiom or usage from the mountains. I've also left in other inconsistencies, hoping to keep the flavor of the story as it flowed out of him, pen to paper: for example, sometimes he writes rank as "Sgt." and sometimes "sergeant." All editorial choices were based upon clearly preserving Dad's voice.

Dr. Howard Davis Grier (David) has written a scholarly foreword that my father would have appreciated very much. His summary of WWII's progress after the entrance of the United States grounds our experience of Herschel's words, setting the geographic and strategic context for them. He also provides the few scholarly corrections and explanations found in [brackets] throughout. For Dr. Grier, reading this memoir was an exciting discovery, a uniquely personal voice adding a treasure trove of on-the-ground reality to his life's work as a historian of the European Theater of Operations in WWII. Thank you, David, for your clarity and compassion.

In this, my father's memoir, you will find the whole, universal soldier's journey: beginning as a callow recruit, becoming a seasoned warrior, leaving the war as a troubled veteran, and creating a life after war. I hope you experience joy, fun, and camaraderie when Dad did, and I hope you find touchstones for understanding, beauty, courage, and healing in these pages.

March 2013

Foreword to the 2013 Edition

As the number of surviving veterans of World War II dwindles, the appearance of new memoirs from participants in that conflict appears less likely. Fortunately, in 1989 Herschel Ponder, from Asheville, North Carolina, felt compelled to put pen to paper to inform his three daughters and grandchildren of his part in the greatest armed struggle of the twentieth century. A broad audience will welcome these well-written and fascinating recollections, which his family has agreed to share with others.

Herschel Ponder's memoirs describe his experiences as a P-47 pilot in the European theater in the final months of World War II. His reminiscences begin in September 1942, when he enlisted in the military at 20 years of age, and end in 1946, shortly after marrying his beloved wife, Eleanor. He joined the US Army Air Corps, as the US Air Force did not exist as a separate branch of service until 1947. In September 1942, while awaiting orders to report for active duty, Ponder attended Clemson Agricultural College (now

Clemson University) in South Carolina, an all-male military institution at the time. He received his call-up early in 1943, and traveled to Miami to an army induction center.

Ponder attended a bewildering array of training programs in Pennsylvania, Texas, Oklahoma, and Virginia before boarding a ship for Great Britain in 1944. He relates several humorous and a few not so humorous experiences from this time, revealing just how dangerous pilot training could be in those days. He clearly loved to fly and quickly learned many maneuvers which would later help to save his life in combat. Upon his arrival in Britain, Ponder was sent to France and joined his unit, the 510th Fighter Squadron of the 405th Fighter Group, part of the Ninth Air Force.

Although not as famous as the US Army Eighth Air Force, which carried out strategic bombing of German industry and transportation, the Ninth Air Force played an equally important role in the defeat of Nazi Germany. The task of Ninth Air Force was primarily to provide close air support to troops at the front, and to bomb and strafe targets behind enemy lines. If American ground forces encountered strong German defensive positions, or if Nazi tank units proved troublesome, American aircraft were called in to attack the Germans from the air. In addition, Ninth Air Force aircraft struck airfields, rail lines, bridges, and supply dumps behind the front. Near the end of the war Ponder stated that he flew missions as far east as Magdeburg on the Elbe River, and as far south as Linz, Austria. Ponder mentions that the 510th Fighter Squadron also provided escorts (protection against German fighter aircraft) for light bombers (A-26 Invaders) on at least one occasion. But most of his missions were to bomb rail lines and motorized columns, hunt enemy tanks, and blow up ammunition dumps.

Because of their mission to furnish close air support, many Ninth Air Force units, such as Ponder's, frequently changed bases as the front advanced. The 405th Fighter Group provided close air support primarily to General George Patton's Third Army. Lieutenant Ponder belonged to the 510th Fighter Squadron, one of three such squadrons in the 405th. Ponder does not give a precise date, but he reached the 510th at St. Dizier, about 120 miles east of Paris, sometime in the fall of 1944, probably in October. The squadron was based in St. Dizier from September 11, 1944 until February 6, 1945.

A brief review of the general course of the war in Western Europe may help to provide the context for Ponder's narrative. Following the D-Day landings on June 6, 1944, the Allies built up their forces in Normandy, and at the end of July they broke out of their beachheads, and liberated Paris in late August. By mid-September the Allies had driven the Germans out of virtually all of France and Belgium, but they had outrun their supplies. Nazi troops still defended most French ports, making supply of Allied forces on the continent extremely difficult. The halt in the Allied advance gave the Germans a chance to re-form their units and to rebuild a line of defense. British commander Field Marshal Sir Bernard Law Montgomery then proposed an ambitious plan to use paratroopers to capture bridges over the Meuse and Rhine Rivers, in hopes of quickly striking into Germany and winning the war by the end of the year. This plan, carried out in mid-September (Operation Market Garden, the subject of the film A Bridge Too Far), failed due to unexpectedly fierce German resistance, and the Allies realized that they still had a difficult struggle ahead of them.

Because of the shortage of supplies there was little change in the situation during October and November. Furthermore, Allied armies in France and Belgium ran up against the West Wall (also known as the Siegfried Line), a belt of fortifications along the German border. The US First Army began a grueling battle along the German-Belgian border for the ancient city of Aachen, the first major German city captured by the Americans, and for the Hürtgen Forest, a horrific struggle which began in mid-September 1944 and continued into February 1945.

On December 16, 1944 Hitler launched the last major German offensive in the west, known to the Germans as the Ardennes Offensive and to Americans as the Battle of the Bulge. Some thirty German divisions, around 200,000 men, attacked American lines in the forests of southern Belgium and Luxemburg with the goal of capturing the port of Antwerp, which had only recently opened to Allied supply ships. Although the German attack caught the Americans by surprise, US troops denied the Germans possession of two vital road junctions, St. Vith (which the Nazis finally seized on December 23) and Bastogne, which the Germans surrounded but never captured. But on December 23 the weather cleared, permitting Allied aircraft to deal punishing blows to German units in the Bulge, and an American attack relieved Bastogne on the 26th. By mid-January 1945, the Germans had been pushed back to their original positions. Ninth Air Force aircraft played a major role in defeating the German offensive, although its squadrons — including Ponder's — suffered heavy losses doing so.

Allied armies launched a series of attacks along the Rhine River in March 1945, and on the 7th American troops captured a bridge intact at Remagen. Patton seized another bridgehead near Oppenheim on March 22, and a few days later British forces launched a major offensive and crossed the Rhine in the north. The German defensive position along the river had collapsed. By April 1 the Americans had surrounded the Ruhr, Germany's major industrial region just east of the Rhine, leading to the surrender of over 300,000 German soldiers. On April 11 American troops reached the Elbe River, the previously decided upon demarcation line between Soviet and Western Allied occupation zones. As the Russians battled their way into Berlin, Anglo-American forces quickly occupied western Germany. Hitler committed suicide on April 30, and the Nazis surrendered on May 8, 1945.

To examine Ponder's specific area of operations, let us look more closely at the activities of Patton's Third Army, which the 510th Fighter Squadron supported, and which played a major role in these campaigns. More so than most other Allied commanders, Patton relied heavily upon tactical

air support, both to strike German forces in his
path as well as for aerial reconnaissance to protect
his flanks from counterattack. Third Army
participated in the later stages of the Allied
breakout from Normandy, and its rapid advance
across northern France aided in trapping several
German divisions with tens of thousands of men in
the Falaise Pocket. The US Third Army reached
and crossed the Seine River before the Germans
could establish a defensive line there, which played
a role in Hitler's decision to retreat from France.
After crossing the Seine, Patton's troops pressed on
to the east into Lorraine. At the end of August,
however, lack of supplies forced Patton to halt his
advance, just short of Metz, which Ponder
mentions was still under German control when he
arrived in St. Dizier. Since Montgomery then
received most of the scarce fuel and ammunition
available to support his airborne operation (Market
Garden), Patton's supply situation did not
improve. Third Army surrounded and besieged
Metz, whose defenders held out until late
November 1944. Elsewhere in Patton's sector, his
units moved up to the German border.

When the Germans launched the Ardennes
Offensive (Battle of the Bulge) in mid-December,
Patton's troops were engaged in bitter fighting
along the West Wall in the Saarbrücken area. In

one of the most difficult and impressive operations of his career, Patton quickly ordered six divisions to disengage, make a ninety-degree turn, and attack to the north against the southern flank of the advancing German armies. With clear weather permitting close air support, Patton's forces advanced rapidly and relieved Bastogne on December 26. He thereby blunted the German offensive only ten days after it had begun.

After halting the German offensive and pushing the Nazis back, Third Army advanced to the Rhine River, once again short of supplies. Patton nonetheless secured a crossing over the Rhine on March 22, 1945 at Oppenheim. In April, Third Army moved across southern Germany and into Austria and liberated Pilsen in Czechoslovakia on May 6, two days before the Germans surrendered. At the end of the war Ponder's squadron was in Kitzingen, in northwest Bavaria.

Lieutenant Ponder's aircraft was the P-47 Thunderbolt, a single engine, propeller-driven fighter bomber that proved mechanically reliable, structurally sturdy, and highly maneuverable. It also was heavily armed, with eight 50 caliber machine guns mounted on the wings, and capable of carrying up to 2,000 pounds of bombs. Ponder flew fifty-one combat missions, mostly in a ground support role, but he often mentions bombing German transportation links and supplies some distance behind the front lines.

Although Ponder expressed great confidence in his P-47, on two occasions he describes encounters with German Me-262s, a new jet aircraft produced near the end of the war. Obviously impressed by their speed, which was unparalleled at the time, he suggests that if the Germans had been able to deploy a good number of these jets as late as September 1944, they could have won the war. While this is possible, it is unlikely. By this stage of the war the Germans were desperately short of fuel, trained pilots, and raw materials. It is impossible to determine whether their use earlier in the war would have been decisive or not, but the American and Soviet economies had the ability to far out-produce German industry. Furthermore, Nazi scientists were nowhere near developing atomic weapons, and if the Germans had held out longer than they did, there is little doubt that Berlin, Munich, or some other German city — rather than Hiroshima — would have been the first to face nuclear destruction.

Ponder describes several close encounters with death. The most constant danger he faced came from heavy anti-aircraft fire, but he also had confrontations with German fighter aircraft. He provides a particularly harrowing account of being shot down by enemy anti-aircraft fire. Mechanical malfunctions were almost as perilous as the Germans, as evidenced particularly in his description of a bomb failing to detach, and having to land with an armed bomb still attached to his wing. "Friendly fire" also posed problems. Once Ponder was almost hit by American artillery shells, and on another occasion bombers flying above him nearly dropped their bombs on his P-47.

Readers of these memoirs will find that they provide more than a depiction of a soldier at war. We also gain a portrait of Herschel Ponder the man, who loved his family and the North Carolina Mountains around his Asheville home. He was a man of faith who enjoyed athletics, hunting and fishing, and who also painted, sang, and acted on stage. He was a Renaissance man. Ponder graduated from high school at age fifteen. By the time he was twenty he had completed two years at Mars Hill Junior College and served two years of a four-year apprenticeship at a Southern Railway shop in Spartanburg, SC, indicating that he possessed mechanical ability as well. It was at this point in his life that he enlisted in the Army Air Corps.

Ponder's memoirs are notable for their honesty. He was not ashamed to admit that he was lonely, or that at times he wanted to cry. He even states that he once tried marijuana, surely an unusual experience for a young man in the 1940s. Furthermore, he was modest. There is no mention of his being awarded the Distinguished Flying Cross and Air Medal, with clusters, or the Purple Heart. In addition, he explains that learning various flying maneuvers saved his life in combat, but he never really clarifies how. He describes several accidents in which he barely escaped death due to mechanical problems or anti-aircraft fire, but his accounts of dogfights with German fighters lack his usual detail. Whether this is due to modesty or his desire not to relive those obviously terrifying encounters is uncertain.

The reminiscences are not without humor. In addition to describing several amusing incidents during training, he also recounts interesting escapades when off duty. When he and his comrades received R & R (rest and recuperation), they often barely avoided trouble with the Military Police. Ponder relates one particularly unusual account from the time immediately after the German surrender. As his unit's recreation officer, it was his duty to improve morale, and he believed that obtaining alcohol would be to the best way to do so. For that reason, he drove from the Austrian border to Belgium, a roundtrip of over 1,000 miles, to obtain several cases of Johnny Walker scotch for his comrades.

When the war ended, Ponder experienced an emptiness and fatigue not unusual for those who endured the stress of prolonged combat and the loss of close friends. He described himself as "an emotional and physical disaster." Although he does not dwell upon it at length, he obviously experienced what is now known as post-traumatic stress disorder after his discharge from the army in October 1945. His transition from "the best exterminator in Europe" and "a professional destroyer" to civilian life as a married university student was disorienting and, at times, jarring. He was shocked by the sudden change to life as a student in Chapel Hill, "where people seemed to play all the time" and "there never seemed to have been a war." Only a few months earlier he had dropped napalm on German soldiers in their trenches, shot up a passenger train, and once he left a whole town in flames. After experiences such as these, how does one so young make the transition to civilian life? At the Christmas Eve midnight church service in 1945, Ponder recalled how he asked God's forgiveness for committing murder. The war made him much more emotional than he had been before the conflict. His wife Eleanor obviously provided him a sense of peace and stability. He also confirmed that it was a cathartic experience for him to write his memoirs, forty-four years after the ordeal of war.

After the war, Ponder completed college at the University of North Carolina at Chapel Hill and then returned to work for Southern Railroad as a supervisor in the maintenance department. Herschel Ponder departed this life on December 16, 2007.

Howard D. Grier, Ph.D.
Erskine College

Ponder Anew

What the Almighty Can Do

For my three girls, Anne, Carol, and Schell

one fine granddaughter,
Kathryn Jeanne Alexander

and one fine grandson,
Samuel Herschel Alexander

On July 4, 1989, I had a sudden urge to tell you about my war, WWII, and the subsequent coping, my peace.

After 45 years some of the events are as vivid as ever, but I don't claim to have total recall. There is no fiction in what is to follow. The times, the places, the people, and the involvements are as I remember them. If my memory is in error, the margin is slight.

DAD

SEPTEMBER 22, 1942.

I was 20 years old.

I enlisted in the Army Air Corps.

When the Japs hit Pearl Harbor, I was seeing a movie in the Plaza Theater, and all at once the screen went blank, the lights came on, and the manager climbed on stage to announce that we, no doubt, were at war.

I was alone. There were voices all around me, but I felt something way deep inside me — an emptiness — possibly dread. My chest felt like it collapsed. There was a shudder. My future, as I had lived my life to then, was doomed. I was caught — caught up in something so vast — so unknown and different. For the moment, I was lost.

But, in the next moment, I was ready; whatever was to come, I'd do the best that I could. No flag waving was necessary. Nothing needed to be said. I was the right age — strong as a mule — healthy as a horse — better prepared than most. I loved my family — all my friends — my home, the town, the mountains — to fish and hunt — and sing with choirs — to paint pictures — and act on stage. For myself and all the things I loved, I had a duty to perform.

CAPT. B. E. KIESLER

Capt. B. E. Kiesler was the Army Air Corps recruiting officer for Western North Carolina. He had been called in service from his job as AG teacher at Valley Springs High School — I had graduated there in 1938, in April, and I was 16 in May. We were such good friends — never had him for a teacher — but we played a lot together. A small group of us, fathers too, strung a net across the gym floor at V.S. — no outside tennis courts — and learned to play the fastest, lowest game of tennis in the world. Fast! The slick hardwood floor allowed little bounce for the ball. It was more like a skip then a bounce. Rarely was a return shot above the waist. We would put the net up in April and take it down in September — 4 months of keen competition; singles matches were great, but the most fun was the doubles — father/son, teacher/ student. Dad and I won most of our matches, especially after I got a Mercer Beasley racket for Christmas.

Anyway, I ran B. E. to death. I'd have sweat dripping off his chin in no time. He'd yell for me to let up a little bit. He was short and I was tall, and

I'd charge the net — drop the return just over the net or slant it away from him.

He had two bird dogs. We lived on Long Shoals Road — nothing like it is now — and there were several coveys of quail close by, a big covey north of our house and two or more across the road, over on Pelzer's estate — CP&L property now. I'd put Wimpy, my most intelligent dog, in the chicken lot, and then the chicken house, garage, or somewhere — so he wouldn't bother B.E.'s bird dogs. It seemed like about every time B.E.'s dogs were set

on some birds, here'd come old Wimp bounding up — with his tongue flashing about — you could see the laugh in his eyes, "I got out again." And B.E. would say, "Not him again." Hunting was over for that time, but we'd set another date.

Herschel and Wimpy

I hadn't seen Capt. Kiesler in over four years. To find him in that recruiting office was a wonderful surprise. Our greetings were most cordial. He took me into his office, and we got caught up on what had happened to each of us. He remembered that I was going to Mars Hill Jr. College. I told him that, after finishing there, I went to Hayne Shop, a Southern Railway shop at Spartanburg, S.C., for a 4-year apprenticeship instead of going onto a 4-yrs. college. After Hayne I would go back to school, study whatever the officials suggested and, more importantly, I would get financial help from the company. My plan would have worked. My record for those first two years was excellent-plus. I knew I was headed to be a big wheel with Southern. Somehow, being in Capt. Kiesler's office made me feel that my railroad career was over.

I took a test he gave me, and I didn't do very well. He said, "Herschel, it will probably be several months until you're called up. You need to go back to school and brush up." I was embarrassed at doing so poorly and said that schools were so crowded (many hoping for an exemption from service) I couldn't get in, especially since classes had begun. He asked if I would go to Clemson. "Sure, anything you say," I said. He picked up the phone, a tall one with the receiver that hung on the side — can't remember if it had a dial. (Clemson was run at that time by career army personnel). "Sergeant, this is Capt. Kiesler in Asheville. Let me speak to Col. Poole. Col., I've got this young man — needs — — can you take care of him?" He turned to me and asked if I could be there in the morning? "Sure can," I said.

My dad and I found the Col.'s office. He shelled out the money, and I was assigned to a barracks and sent straight to supply to get my uniforms — light blue shirts, blue coats and pants, black shoes, cap with a black visor, and a black wide belt. I changed into the uniform, and my Dad took what I was wearing back home. I matriculated within the next hour and attended my first class that afternoon.

Clemson had hazing.

It was awful.

Freshmen were called rats. I was a bo-rat, but lived with 4 other freshmen. I had been given a numeral 2, instead of 3 — my academic rank — so I would have to go through the hazing. Freshmen were 1's. There were some, not all, of the upper classmen that were pure mean. They treated the freshmen like dogs — both mentally and physically. My four roommates' butts were black and blue and green from the beatings that they constantly took. Somebody might have thought it was funny, but I thought it was sadistic. I was fortunate. No one laid a hand or board on me. I was the same age as the seniors and as physically strong as any of them.

I was polite — tried to stay out of the line of fire — obeyed orders — and was very quiet. To this day I doubt that I would have taken one of those beatings. I guess it showed, because they didn't try. The army was much easier.

We drilled and paraded — over and over again. Retreat parade — Monday through Thursday — was, at times, very stirring. The Clemson Band would usually be on the parade ground in front of the old buildings, practicing. Each barracks had its own cadet commander. He had a staff — Lord, did they prance. Each commander wanted his to be the best. We'd fall out on the courtyard — form up — count off in our squads — be inspected for dress — and off we'd go at a fast clip — some companies ahead — others behind. We were "B" Company. The band was playing now. There were two battalions in the regiment. All of that maneuvering of companies into their proper place in their battalion at the right distances without a hitch was quite an accomplishment — kinda like watching a ballet. All were at attention — interminably. The grand poobah cadet of the regiment would bark an order to his second in command — staff formed in front of him — second would approach — salute — say something — about face after another salute and bark something at his corps — all saluted — and he marched them over to each battalion — go through some ritual — regiment to battalion to company and in reverse — all the way back again to the big mogul — "All present and accounted for, Sir." Then he'd yell something else — dialect like no other — and the honor guard would appear. After what seemed like interminable instructions, the Honor Guard would march to the flagpole — go through a ritual and two cadets would get ready to lower the flag. A roll of drums and the "Star Spangled Banner." It would raise the hair on your head, especially when one or more trumpets would top out at the end. At attention all this time, there were those that would pass out. Down they'd go — some stiff as a board. The cadets on each side could carry them to the rear and return to their places. Then, we would pass in review out past the mogul and staff and regular army personnel. Retreat wasn't easy — rather an ordeal — but what respect for our flag — and what Prussian accomplishments.

Then, there was the drill team. What a magnificent display of intelligence, stamina, and coordination. We could hear them practicing before daylight and after dark, and see them at times during the day. Their pace was fast — impossibly fast. At full speed they could stop on a dime — make turns — about face — go off in all directions — and return. The precision was awesome. Their most difficult maneuver, to me, was the Queen Anne's salute, where cadets would be going in four directions — twirl their rifles over their shoulders and, as the butt of the rifle touched the ground, so would the cadet's knee. Then, after a significant pause, the rifles were twirled back over the shoulder as the cadet arose and his first step was at full speed again. This, when used, was always the finale and off the field they'd go.

We all learned and did close order drill — formations — inspections — fall out — each cadet took his assigned place — put his left arm out to the side and spaced off — the second row, after spacing sideways, spaced behind the first line etc. Attention! Count off. Right face! Forward March — hut two three four. Squad halt — one two. Men, listen! It's about time you learned your right foot from your left — etc. Pay attention. We'll stay out here all night, if we have to.

Each barracks had its own little drill team — a star for the barracks cadet officer, if they were good.

There were four of us at Clemson from Asheville — Pete Parthemus, George Karambolis, Charles Moody and I. We'd thumb home just about every weekend, particularly to get something good to eat. No problem getting a ride — with the Clemson uniform on. We could sign out after our last class of the week — so we didn't come home together, but most of the time we'd go back together. Pete's uncle ran a restaurant in West Greenville on the road to Clemson, and if we didn't have a ride by the time we walked that far (traffic generally runs north & south or east & west — our ride would let us out in Greenville somewhere and we'd start walking west), we'd stop in. The first time I ordered a ham omelet and a glass of milk. Pete's uncle tried his best to make me eat something else — pie or something. But I didn't. After I was finished, I climbed off the stool at the counter and went to the cash register to pay my bill. Pete ran up and turned me around and said, "Don't do that. You'll hurt his feelings." Pete and his uncle would always hug one another, and give the other three of us a good handshaking. Sure were nice people.

Pete told me one day the greatest insult to a Greek was to put your hand straight out toward his face and turn the palm up. That meant he was a S.O.B., and you'd better be ready for a fight.

Nick, Pete's father, ran a restaurant down on Depot Street near the Southern Railway passenger depot. That place was full of railroad men 24 hours a day. Nick had to be pretty tough because in the steam engine days railroaders were a bunch of tough customers.

Pete became a navy pilot, and I heard he was sent out from the carrier past his range, failed to rendezvous and was lost at sea.

George was a brain. Straight "As" and in Physics? I heard he got shot up in Italy, and now lives in Virginia.

Moody, never heard about him again.

Classes at Clemson were a big drag for two reasons: First the professors I had were mighty puny: I had had wonderful teachers at Mars Hill. Second, I expected to be called into service any day — lots of the boys were. Which makes me think of a little blond-headed boy — about 5'6" — an upperclassman that had been in ROTC training beginning with high school. He had already been commissioned a 2nd Lt. The day he got his orders to report for duty, he went to Col. Poole's office and told the sergeant that he wanted his discharge papers from Clemson. The sergeant said he couldn't give him his discharge without his parents' consent. Whereupon he went back to his room — put on his 2nd Lt. Uniform — went back to the sergeant and said, "Sergeant, give me my discharge papers." And the sergeant said, "Yes Sir, Lt."

The semester ended sometime in mid-January, and I didn't want to go back. My Mom and Dad gave me the arguments why I should start the second semester. I gave in and did, but my heart sure wasn't in it. One afternoon into the second week I cut my classes — something I had never intentionally done before — thumbed over to Seneca and saw "The Black Swan" with Errol Flynn. That weekend when I went home, my Dad said, "Well, Bud, your number's come up. A man over in Tennessee saw your name on a list. We'll go down to Clemson tomorrow and get your things."

The few days at home, I visited most of my kinfolks, played with my good ole dog — Wimpy — and ate all the good food I could hold.

My orders came. Mom and Dad took me down to the train station — said my goodbyes — hugged my Mom one last time — got on the train, the Carolina Special, and was on my way to Miami Beach.

A P. S. from Clemson: When I went to Chapel Hill after the war, every credit from Mars Hill transferred, but not a single one from Clemson did.

MIAMI BEACH

I was on my way to what? Lord, I was lonesome. I wanted to cry so bad it hurt. I was a man. I couldn't. I'd look out the window — then at the ceiling, take a deep breath — look at my orders. I thought of old Wimpy — how we'd hunt quail together — and rabbits. When I would catch one in my rabbit gum, I'd make Wimpy sit still until I turned the rabbit loose right in front of him — yip yip yip as he carried that rabbit into the pine thicket. I'll bet he's the only part collie-part German police that ever learned to track rabbits in the whole world.

Then, I thought about the boys at Clemson — what was happening to them.

I was in the Army Air Corps — Air Force came later. Would I fly? And in what? The only plane I had ever flown in was a tri-motor Ford — at Carrier Field in Asheville — probably about 14 years old, me, that is.

I didn't know what time it was. I didn't bring my watch with me. We stopped at stations — some would get off — not many — and lots more would get on. I looked out the window at the trees and fields passing by — for a good long time — and then — thought — I'll just eat this lunch my Mom packed for me.

Miami Beach was one efficient operation — an induction center. You never saw so many people. There were GI busses to greet us in Miami at the train station. The ride over to the beach was just beautiful. I had never seen a place so elegant. Large hotels — apartments — businesses, some white, but a lot of pastels — lots of grass and well-kept shrubbery. I saw a flock of flamingos as we crossed the causeway — large, beautiful, pink birds. I had never seen anything like that. The busses pulled up in front of the Hotel Flamingo. Even with all the inductees around, you could see lots of evidence that it was an elegant place. As we unloaded off the bus there was a small, dark skinned, black haired sergeant that said, "Youse guys stand over there." He had the thickest New York City accent I had ever heard. We formed up and marched to the Ken-Mae Apartments, our home. Before we were assigned a room, the sergeant gave us an orientation speech — what he expected out of us — where we'd eat — and how we'd march to get there — how we'd dress — what time we'd be waked up — what time to fallout. "And Youse guys are going to learn close order drill, and we're going to retreat parade every day. Now, these are the guys that are going to be in charge of youse, and youse do what they say — all the time. This is Cpl.(?), Cpl.(?), Cpl.(?), and Cpl. Grogan." Naturally, I drew Grogan, one of the most detestable people I ever met. He was so obnoxious that I'd have to clench my fists to keep from hitting him. I figured he was sick in the head until I realized he was just bucking for sergeant stripes. He was my first experience of what some people would do to get ahead in the army. I met lots more and avoided every one of them I could.

"Now, weeze going to form youse up into squads and that's your place while youse is here," the sergeant said. Your place in a squad was assigned by how tall you were — tallest first and on down to the least tall — or shortest. Grogan took our squad out in the street to teach us how to drill. Then the most fantastic thing happened — we lined up — spaced off — and stood at attention. We realized that most all of us were from Clemson. The look on Grogan's face was pure amazement. Later, we found that the sergeant was dumbfounded. A few days later, while sitting on the grass outside the apartment, the sergeant said, "Youse is the best bunch of guys I've ever seen. I want to make a deal with youse. You take care of me, and I'll take care of youse. I'd like to form a drill team and be the best platoon on the beach. When we go to the Flamingo to eat, we'll put on a show for all these turkeys. Now, youse come up with a good drill team, stay out of trouble, and I'll get us out of every retreat parade that I possibly can. I'll schedule all the places you got to be during that time." We did, and he did.

Retreat Parade was an ordeal — the few we attended, anyway. Same old thing — we formed into squads — then platoons — then companies, then battalions, then regiments — and marched and marched to a golf course a mile or two away — a complete sea of people. We would have to stand at attention so long that lots of men would pass out. Some would kind of crumple down easy — some would get a knee down and go over sideways — and some would stay as stiff as a board until they hit face down. It wasn't like Clemson — no help — they lay where they were.

I never did pass out — there or anywhere else. It's basically a matter of breathing properly so that your heart would pump enough blood up into your head. In addition some of us would wet our handkerchiefs in cold or ice water — make a pad and put it on top of our heads under our caps. And if we were wearing white gloves, we'd dip them too. One Clemson boy next to me hit face down —

eyes, nose, and mouth full of dirt — developed trench mouth — went to the hospital — we never saw him again. This happened all through my time in service. It was something you learned to expect, but something you didn't always forget. His name I don't remember — where we were — his face — his blond hair — his lean body, I do. I have wondered whatever happened to him and others too.

We marched everywhere — to get a physical — to the dentist — to get our shots — to take tests — to see V.D. films — to supply — to the barber — and, to eat at the Flamingo. My luck was still holding out. I was too tall for the drill team. I would have stuck out like a sore thumb. Our team was good — fast clip — good moves — solid unity — just great. They'd get enthusiastic applause every night before supper. You talk about proud! Our sergeant grinned from ear to ear, but he or the Cpl's didn't even attempt to lead the team. One of our own was drill master.

After standing in line — there were always lines to everything — I finally got to the door of the building to get my physical. There was an aisle through the building with a doctor's cubicle every so often. As I moved down the aisle one doctor would do one thing — next doctor another thing. I finally got to one that listened to my chest. He had me step into his cubicle and sit down — and he listened some more. He got up and left and came back with a second doctor and was telling him he thought he had one with a heart murmur. After listening, the second doctor left and came back with an older doctor, who listened and announced, "That's not a heart murmur — just a thin chest wall. He'll make a damn good pilot." Somewhere along that line I stepped up on a scales and the doctor asked me what I wanted to fly. I said, "Fighter Plane." He hit me in top of the head with the measuring bar and told the person next to him, "Six feet." I was actually 6 ' 2."

Another time — a line — shots. Line moved pretty fast. Lord, those shots — looked like horse doses. There was a shooter on each side of the line. It took a lot of courage — even bravery — to last this line out. It's a good thing we had our physicals first. One doctor asked each one if he had ever fainted — if yes, we heard you were shipped out somewhere else. As we went through the door we were told to take our fatigues off down to the waist. Then, on each side of the line there was a person with a paint bucket and a two inch brush used to paint our upper arms. Looked like iodine — brownish yellow. The odor in the whole building — disinfectants and ethers — was stifling. We could see what was happening ahead. The shooters would put a hand under each arm near the armpit and spear the big upper muscle with the shot. The reason they put one hand under the arm was to keep the shootee from falling when he fainted. I never saw so many boys pass out in my life — some even before they got to the shooters. Medical attendants were close on each side of us and would catch him and walk him up to the shooters in his turn and hand him over to others who walked him (or drug his feet) outside and laid him down on a concrete driveway. Others made it outside before passing out. That driveway was full of people that were down. I don't mean that everyone passed out — I didn't — but the number was amazing. I felt a little light headed — put my head between my knees and was ok in about a minute. All through service we had to get booster shots — never in conditions like that. Anyway, I never heard of anyone getting tetanus, cholera, typhus, or anything we got shots for.

Another day we were taken — marched to a theater where we had to see a V.D. film. You would think we were a bunch of sissies — which we sure weren't. They showed advanced stages of gonorrhea and syphilis. A few boys passed out and one two seats over from me peed in his britches. Sure was a terrible film to look at.

There were other days in various theaters or buildings that we were given intelligence tests. I was a little apprehensive having done — or at least felt I had done — poorly on the test Captain Kiesler gave me.

Which brings up Cpl. Grogan, again! I suppose the poor fellow wasn't over-blessed. When he would make us drill unnecessarily, or have us down on our hands and knees mowing the grass blade by blade with our fingers — picking up match stems, cigarette butts — or something, we decided to play with him. We'd be marching-hut, two, tree, fo he'd say — and the rear half of the squad would about face and off they'd go to his cadence — "but we heard you say about face." Finally, some would break ranks and run to hide — behind shrubbery, telephone poles, apartment — somewhere. When he'd go off to find them, the rest of us would hide. One day some of us dashed into the front bedroom. There were two single beds still in the room. I got under one — someone else under the other one — and one boy climbed up on the closet shelf — a real acrobatic achievement. The sideboard of the bed was so low I had to lie down on my back and squirm as far as I could under and then lift the bed to get my head under. Very uncomfortable. To turn my head after I was all the way under I'd have to lift the box springs — and my feet were spread-eagled. Well, old "Grog" came in. I could see his feet walking around. He'd stand and study. Went to the closet — the door was open — looked inside — didn't find anybody — finally left the room. About 15 minutes he was back again — same routine. This time while looking in the closet — he looked up. Well, that boy yelled real loud — dropped to the floor and ran out the door. Old Grog was so startled he didn't even give chase. My other bed buddy and I stayed under the beds until we heard a "fall-in." We nonchalantly took our places.

Another time — 6 of us each took a book or magazine and at the first opportunity made for the storage room in the back of the apartment. We went in — closed the door — turned on the one light by its pull string — got us a seat — and read — quiet as could be. The path to the door was chat and would make a crunch when walked on. The top half of the door was latticed — couldn't see in but we could see 45 degrees out. Sure enough — after a long time — we heard Old "Grog's" crunch. We pulled the light out and got ready and when he turned the door knob — we charged — knocked him on his ass and ran right over the top of him — around to the front — dropped to our hands and knees — started clipping grass — and slowly old "Grog" came into view. He looked and looked — oh how he wanted just one of us! In our fatigues — we all looked alike.

The KenMae Apartments were on a cross street —
one street over from the beach. Even though it was
early February, some of us would occasionally go
swimming in the surf. The water was not really
cold. The Gulf Stream must have been pretty close
to shore. One thing that wasn't very nice about the
swim was that when we got out we would have
from specks to globs of black oil on us. Every out-
going tide would leave an oily band on the beach.
We knew a lot of ships were being sunk — the
German U-boats were taking a heavy toll. On some
days I could see ships out on the horizon, and I'd
get kind of a sinking feeling inside, wondering
which ships, if any, would make it through the
night. The beach was always blacked out every
night — no lights anywhere. We knew that it was
so we couldn't be detected from the ocean, but
more importantly, so that our ships would not be
silhouetted for the German subs.

One important thing happened at Miami Beach — I
found out what my true shoe size was. My
problem was that my left foot was 11 AA and my
right foot — 10A — and a 10½A — logical of
course — would let each foot adapt to the shoe.
Breaking in a new pair of shoes wasn't easy. I'd
wear two pairs of socks that on occasion I would
dampen. The moisture made the leather more
pliable, and the double sock prevented blisters.

21

There is no better friend than a pair of shoes that fit and are comfortable — especially when you know you are walking or running around the world.

One last comment about our sergeant — we rarely saw him. He was there — and took over — every time he should have — never knew where he stayed — but that "old boy" sure did get a lot of sack time. He knew a good thing when he saw it — us — and he made the best of it. He was smart. He was straight forward with us — no bull s___, honest with us. He trusted us — and we him. One day, near the last, he said "Youse is the best bunch I ever had."

We packed our duffle bags — loaded on busses at the Flamingo — returned across the causeway to the train station in Miami — loaded onto day coaches (our destination must be near) and left Miami to somewhere. There's always some dumb-bunny in the chain of command in the army (I never did figure out for sure whether it came from the top — middle — or bottom) that says — don't tell them anything — give them their latrine breaks — and three meals a day. When we get there — act — follow command. Don't think — don't question — just follow any orders given.

What a hell of a way to run an army. It's really dishonest. You know that somewhere you're likely to have to follow a nit wit — — — — or be one yourself.

That train trip was hard on me — mentally. I was too apprehensive — where're we going — what kind of place will it be — wonder what the airfield will look like. After the third day on that coach about all I could think of was when are they going to let us off this thing. When we left Miami, I would have bet we would end up in Georgia somewhere, but here it was three days later and we were near Cincinnati, Ohio. It had been a long, slow trip, so far. It seemed we never did go very fast, and there were a lot of stops. Seemed like we were always changing train crews, or swapping steam engines, or watering the engine tender from a watering tank, or sitting on a siding to let another train pass, or just sitting.

There were sounds at night, when most everyone was quiet, that one didn't pay attention to in the day time — the clickety-click of the wheels passing over rail joints, the wheels singing when rounding a curve, the sound of air escaping and the thuds and tightening of the brake rigging when the engineer applied the brakes, the grinding sound the brake shoes made on the wheels, the faint sound of the whistle when he blew for a crossing, and when there were crossing gates the clang,

clang, clang of the crossing bell, and sometimes, when stopped, the beating of metal with a hammer under the car.

The coach we were on was up-to-date. It had good reclining seats that would turn in the opposite direction, and this allowed two seats to face each other. At night we would put duffle bags between the seats until it was level and three of us could sleep together — the one in the middle with his head where the other two's feet were. Others slept on duffle bags where there was enough room to throw one down — bulkheads, lavatories, or anyplace.

We had a kitchen car — made out of a baggage car — in the middle of the train, where cooks prepared two meals a day. When it came our turn to eat, we would make our way through the other coaches — enter the mess car — dip our mess kit and mess cup in a tub of boiling water — get our food served — and return to our car. Food is served in the army in a mess tent — mess hall — or mess car. I soon realized where the word mess came from — everything in your mess kit ran together.

We passed Cincinnati sometime after dark, and the next morning we were in some mountains. I was lost. Mountains in Ohio? I tried to orient myself, but with all the curves my good sense of direction completely failed me. Sometime up in the day we pulled to a stop and someone shouted, "Everybody out," the sign on the end of the depot said, Clarion, PA.

Clarion State Teacher's College. No air base? What gives? We were going to school — and — we were now aviation cadets. The army had commandeered Clarion — no one but us. There were 300 of us. We were divided into quintiles — ranked 1 through 300 as a result of the tests done in Miami Beach. There would be a quintile leaving at the end of each month for the training command. "Cadet Moon (as I remember), you scored the highest and will command this entire unit while you are here. The cadets in the first quintile are: 2 so and so, 3, 4 — ." I was number 19; 19 out of mostly college students. I felt such relief. Capt. Kiesler's test was still eating on me. I was not a dumb bunny — and I knew the other 299 were not either. That's the first time in my life that I learned the true meaning of the word "humble." And at the same time I went around smiling at everybody because it was coming from inside.

We had all kinds of courses — English, history, math, science, and some I don't remember.

Our history professor was a small, baggy suited, graying, bespectacled man, who was just marvelous. He said, "Gentlemen, I am dumbfounded. I have been given an impossible task. I have to teach you World History in seven days, and, by God, I'm going to have a stab at it!" He passed out a black bound history book nearly three inches thick — gave us about ten minutes to read the introduction, and said, "I have divided this book into the most important periods of man's existence, and in each period I will point out the most significant events that have brought us to where we are today." He told us that the first period would include "so many chapters — to turn to page so and so — now to page so and so — hold your fingers in these pages — and page so and so. These three events are closely related because — — " those seven days were unbelievably exciting. He was super!!!

Our English teacher looked like a Wagnerian soprano — tall — large wind chest, but quite handsome. As we were taken with the history professor, she was taken with us. One of the first things she assigned was to write a short paper on an incident or something that had affected our lives. "Music in my life," or something close was my topic. She had each one of us to come up front and read our paper to the rest of the class, much of the time she stood up — only a few feet from the person reading. She didn't want to miss a word. When I finished reading, I looked at her, and with tears in her eyes, she said, "Beautiful, just beautiful." She had nothing but praise for each paper read. When we were done, she stood before us in silence for some time, handkerchief in hand — occasionally dabbing her nose — teary-eyed, and then said, "This class has been the greatest teaching experience of my whole career. You young men are so intelligent, wonderful, and you've made me love each one of you. I wish my association with you would never end. "

I figured there were two reasons for her emotional tears — pure joy and her perception of what was to happen to us after we left Clarion.

Within a day or two after we arrived in Clarion, the body of Clarion's first war casualty arrived. The people in Clarion seemed to be civic-minded, close-knit, and very patriotic. Some of the WWI vets approached our cadet commander and asked for an honor guard for the funeral. Six of the tallest cadets were picked — also a trumpet player. We had no rifles, so the vets scrounged up six relics. We had no idea what we were to do. A vet named Musi was making all the impromptu arrangements, and since I was the tallest cadet and leader of the squad, Musi and I became good friends.

We started the procession at the funeral home. The pallbearers placed the casket on a flatbed wagon.

Three flag bearers were first — then the caisson next (casket flag-draped) — the honor guard and then the vets with some part of a uniform on — a coat or cap or leggings — not a complete uniform in the bunch. From the funeral home we went down a hill on Main Street — all the way through town — and turned up a hill to the cemetery. As we passed through the main town, people were lined up on each side of the street — at attention — with hats off — some with little flags — and deathly quiet — except for the ominous clanking of the steel-tired wagon wheels on the cobble stones.

At the grave side the honor guard lined up — at attention — on the side opposite of the grave from the family. After the graveside rites, Musi nodded his head, and I said, "Present arms! Ready! Aim! Fire!" About 4 of the six rifles fired. "Load! Ready! Aim! Fire!" Two fired. The last time one fired.

Our little blond-headed trumpet man had gone over the hill out of sight. One of the old vets played taps and after each phrase would wait for that echo that was out of sight — a moment that would wring any man's heart out.

Musi came up to me after the family had left and with tears still in his eyes asked me to come to supper at their house. I accepted, and told another cadet to tell our commander where I was. Musi had a dry cleaning business on Main Street and lived in an apartment above. I met his wife and high school age daughter, and both were wonderful. His wife had prepared one of her Italian specialties — with chicken — mmmm — good. And the daughter got the family album out and showed me pictures of her older brother, who was in service somewhere. When Musi poured our second glass of wine, we went to the kitchen table to have, for me, one delicious dinner.

I was invited to dinner there 3 or 4 more times. By the end of the 2nd I was no longer a guest, but a member of the family.

Frank Onco was the cadet impresario. He got the idea to have a talent show. He got all the skits and acts together, invited the college faculty, and was the M.C. — that evening was something else. With his easy gab he kept everything moving and entertaining. Near the end of the program, Frank said, "There's a cadet out in the audience that doesn't know that he's on the program. Cadet Ponder, please come to the stage." I almost slid down out of my seat. Everyone started clapping — so, I got up and went to the stage. I got in Frank's ear and asked him what in the hell he was doing. Ignoring me he said, "The only practice we've had is in the shower." I whispered to him, "Frank, you know it'll sound awful with just the lead and the bass part. Find us a tenor." After a few mmmm's to get our pitch and no further introduction, we burst forth with "This is my country." Frank lead — and me, bass (which I'd learned singing with the Spartanburg Male Chorus). When we finished — all hell broke loose — they cheered — they clapped — they whistled, stood up, stomped. It went on forever, it seemed. Shook hands with Frank and started to leave the stage — and it doubled. Frank ran over and pulled me back — can you sing so & so, or so & so. Then, we'll just do it again. I said, "The audience, too." By being so spontaneous that song grabbed us all. When I returned to my seat, I didn't see many dry eyes — including my own.

At a little grass airfield nearby, where there were several Piper Cubs and the like, each one of us got about a ten minute ride. The pilots were local civilians, and mine, after we had climbed to about 500 feet, asked me where the airport was. I pointed to it, and he smiled. It is a different world up there.

I could never forget Clarion — the time, the place, the people — the fun we all had — and how eager I was.

I got my orders. The Gulf Coast command — some went to the Southeast. I was to report to SAAC Center, Kelly Field, San Antonio, Texas.

SAAC CENTER

There are no fond memories of that place. SAAC Center was a compound west of San Antonio — I never saw Kelly Field — that held thousands of cadets waiting to be shipped out to pilot, navigator or bombardier training, or regular army, or whatever. The army called it preflight. I called it a prison. A high, 9 or 10 foot fence went around the perimeter that had 5 strands of barbed wire on top of that — and guards at every gate. I spent 13 weeks in that place before they let me have a one-day pass to San Antonio, and even that morning we had to run a 4 to 6 mile obstacle course. It was hot. It was miserable. It was dusty. It was boring. That's the first time I heard the expression, "No happiness allowed."

It was common knowledge to never volunteer for anything in the army, but at our first formation, I did. The egotistical — washed out — Captain in charge said, "I need a volunteer that has some mechanical knowledge." I didn't hesitate. I stepped forward. "Lt. get his name and have him report to me" — — "Are there any others that have mechanical aptitude?" Three others stepped forward. "Lt. find three wheel barrows and have these three men engineer these piles of rocks just behind us across the parade ground to that pile on the other side." My luck had held out one more time.

I reported to the Captain. The sergeant in the outer office went to the captain's door, "Cadet Ponder reporting, sir." "Send him in." I was impressed — with all the stacks of papers around — with the neatness of his office. "Cadet, there are lots of repairs to be made in our barracks — broken windows, door hinges and locks, etc. Can you repair them?" "Yes sir." "Turn a weekly progress report into my sergeant, outside." "Yes sir." "Dismissed." I did an about face and departed. I felt my face flush. I had a case of the frantics — no tools, no nothing. I had told the captain I could do the impossible? As I passed the sergeant, I laid out my problem. He smiled — wrote me a note — and said, "Take this to supply. They'll help you." I made lots and lots of repairs — a whole slew of two-story barracks to take care of.

I still had to do what all the others did — the running — calisthenics — classes — films. But there were times — in my favor. Very few times did I make special formations or that damn daily retreat parade. The Miami Beach sergeant taught me well.

Running. Almost a matter of survival. Never less than 4 miles — on occasion up to 8 miles — into ravines — and out again — back down again — sometimes on hands and knees, if you didn't keep up, you ended up on KP (kitchen patrol) or many hours of marching on the parade ground. Rumor had it that a boy went down (another company), was taken to the infirmary — and died. They busted his heart. He was the sixth.

My mother and father begged enough gas coupons and came to see me in that awful place. I was so glad to see them. I was told to report to the chaplain's office, I had visitors. We met in the chapel. Bless their hearts. To see them almost did me in. Home. I hadn't had much time to think of home.

On Sundays I sang in the choir — about 30 cadets directed by a cadet who was a real musician — a superb director. The choir met one hour before service for rehearsal. Besides the regular hymns, we did some rather wonderful anthems — the one I remember most was "The Storm is O'er" set to Lohengrin. We basses outdid ourselves.

After 13 weeks, after running 4 miles, eight of us got a pass to San Antonio. We had heard that the White Plaza Hotel was where the good food was. We were seated at a round table. I asked the waitress what was the best steak. She said "Porterhouse." That's what all eight ordered — most like me — rare. After what seemed a long time she came back to the table and said they were out — rationing, you know — but that they could substitute baby beef. We said to go for it. My eyes popped open. That steak literally hung over the side of my plate. We were in Texas and things are big — but what would a steak look like from one of their steers? It was delicious — and every time we got a pass, the White Plaza was our first stop — mostly 10:30 to 11:00 a.m.

Finally, orders — to primary flight training.

CIMMARON FIELD - OKLAHOMA CITY

We left SAAC Center in old straight-backed coaches that must have been stored in a siding somewhere for years. I was in the last coach. We opened all the windows that would open — still hot — and opened the rear door. The smoke and cinders from the steam engine poured in on us, and the dust boiled in from the road bed. It wasn't long before we looked like a bunch of coal miners — still beat walking.

Cimmaron Field was an uptown place — pretty well kept. Civilians did most of the work, including the cooking and serving of food. The field was exactly one mile square. In fact, most of the prairie states are laid out in one mile squares running north and south and east and west. A perfect place to learn to fly.

I didn't know anyone now. All the friends I'd made at Miami Beach, Clarion, and SAAC Center were somewhere else. The army had some sort of a master plan to keep friends from staying together. Each unit had last names beginning from A to Z. If all last names began with S, there would be great confusion. Then, each unit would have boys from as many states as possible. I never met another cadet from North Carolina through all my flying training.

No time was wasted. We were split into two sections — one section on the flight line from 12NOON to 12NOON — one section in the classroom 12NOON to 12NOON alternating with each other. Same way — all through training.

The classroom work was very intensive. We learned Morse code — all about weather, maps, atmospheric pressures, isobars, fronts, cloud formations, falling weather, how an Aneroid Barometer reacted to different pressures (to find later that's what an altimeter was in an aeroplane). Maps again — we studied the differences between Mercator, lambert, and conical maps. Atmosphere — the make-up, oxygen, nitrogen, the effects on the body, density, free falling bodies, the difference when in a vacuum. We would have all made good weather men.

Aerodynamics, what made a plane fly, the camber of the leading-edge of the wing, how the longitudinal, horizontal, and vertical axis had to have the correct relationship, the effect of the movable surfaces, ailerons, elevators, and rudder — and on and on.

Engines — what happens to make the propeller turn. All our engines were piston engines. The Germans developed a jet engine near the end of the war — also a solid fuel engine.

The propeller was fastened to the crankshaft which was eccentric where the connecting rods went to the pistons. The pistons were in a cylinder with a firing chamber at the top — which had an intake and exhaust valve. The piston made two complete strokes in one cycle — compression stroke and exhaust stroke. In the compression stroke the magneto fired (both valves closed) two degrees before the piston reached top dead center allowing longer burning of the fuel mixture — more power. Even then, much of the mixture is exhausted before it is fully burned (exploded). When the piston reaches the bottom of the cylinder, the exhaust valve opens and as the piston rises, it pushes the unspent mixture out. As the piston starts down the exhaust valve closes, and the intake valve opens to allow the fuel that has been mixed with air in the proper proportion in the carburetor to enter the cylinder. When the piston reaches the bottom — the intake valve closes, and the chamber is ready for the compression stroke again. (Later, when flying a P-47 in combat, water was added to the mixture in the carburetor from a 15 gal. and then a 30 gal tank. With everything full forward — the throttle, the mixture passed a mechanical stop, and the turbo, a solenoid switch on top of the throttle handle was turned on, allowing water to enter the mixture. The water cooled the mixture down — the engine quit blowing back smoke, and the plane felt like something kicked it in the butt. Not only did the water cool the mixture, but also turned to steam in the cylinder — thus, a gas and steam engine at the same time. The power created was fantastic).

THE FLIGHT LINE

At last — airplanes — a low wing monoplane — the PT (Fairchild) 19, ranger engine. From this point on, I, and all the other cadets, were totally consumed with learning to fly — on the flight line — during meals — at breaks between classes — and after supper until sack time. In the barracks we would gather in small groups and go over everything that happened that day. What did your instructor say? We had civilian instructors. Did he let you taxi? What RPM was used to taxi? Where was the stick? Could you see straight ahead? We zigzagged. Could you tell any difference when he checked both mags — magnetos? What was the air speed when you left the runway? The RPM? Boy, did you feel that torque? How much right rudder did he use? How high did you climb? Did he do any turns? At what airspeed? Did you see all those planes in the landing pattern? Wasn't that first leg 45 degrees downwind? Second leg — straight downwind? Base leg — crosswind? What was the airspeed on the landing leg? How much flaps did he use? How hard did you hit?

This went on and on. I was beginning to take over the controls, and it wasn't long before I was shooting landings with the instructor. One day, the instructor and I were walking toward our plane and, all at once he stopped — turned — and real ugly — said, "I'm tired flying with you. I'm fed up. Don't know whether you'll ever make a pilot or not. You go on by yourself. I'm not going." As I was passing him, he very gently asked, "Do you think you can take off and land by yourself?" "Yes, sir," I said. I soloed!

After that, all I got was a check ride, now and then. He'd tell me to go out to a road crossing we'd been using and practice my turns — figure 8s, etc. and that I'd better have them perfect when he checked me again. The same was true for stalls, and dead engine spins, and over the top spins — over the top was the most fun — with power on I'd go into a severe right or left turn — the stick back in my belly — the inside wing would stop flying — the outside wing still be flying — would jerk the lower wing up and over the top — and I'd be headed straight down in a very tight spin. I'd pop the stick forward — hit the opposite rudder — to break the spin — and come out the bottom. I got so that I could come out of a spin in any direction — the way I was headed — 180 degrees — or in between.

When I went out to practice, I religiously did what the instructor told me. In fact, I always felt that he was in the other cockpit. After I was satisfied for his check, I would try to do the things we cadets had talked about in the barracks — things that the instructor had not taught yet. How do you do a half roll? Pull the nose above the horizon — a little right stick and right rudder (power on) — at 45 degrees rudders neutral — then, left rudder hard (to hold nose up at 90 degrees) start pushing the stick forward — begin to let up on left rudder — and when upside down — the rudder neutral and the stick well forward the engine would quit — float type carburetor — reverse the process with stick and rudder — level again — the engine would catch up — and I'd be off to another project — a complete roll, or a loop. But that half roll took numerous times. About half way through the maneuver I would slide out — sideways — lose altitude — climb back and try again. When I finally got on my back, I'd slide out on the reverse process. It was kinda like rubbing your stomach in a circle and patting the top of your head. But! I did it!

One day, on a check ride, the instructor said that he was going to show me a half roll. "Now, you do it," he said. I laid that S.O.B. over — held the nose up several seconds after the engine quit — and brought her back level. The instructor let out a war whoop — beat the side of the plane with his hands, and said, "I don't believe it. You can't do that." (Actually, mine was better than his.) "Can you do that again?" "Yes sir." I did!

Another day — I had learned to do a loop in the barracks — I decided to do a loop. A plane is designed so that at cruising speed all the controls are neutral — when slower, right rudder — when faster, left rudder — otherwise you couldn't fly a straight line. I had everything worked out — air speed — dive to a certain speed — keep on line with rudder — pull stick back smoothly — go over the top — relax stick — nothing to it. Except! In my barracks training, one of those other cadets forgot to tell me to increase the throttle on the way up. Well, everything was going perfectly on the up leg, when all at once I realized the plane had all but quit flying — I kicked right rudder — left rudder — jerked the stick into my belly (which is just natural when in trouble) and NOTHING happened. I was suspended in nothingness — half on my back in the top half — and nothing. Then I very slowly began to descend — backwards. With the stick in my gut the first flying surface to take effect was the elevators (on the tail). It was like — crack the whip. There was the awfulest, most violent snap as the rest of that plane (open cockpit) plunged downward. It threw me against my safety belt until later I found blue places on each hip. I knew a plane was not designed to fly backwards. I knew something had to be damaged. At straight and level I eased back on the throttle — worked my tail controls — the rudder and elevators. Everything seemed all right. I eased into the traffic pattern — gently landed that plane — walked away from it, and hoped I would never get that one again.

That night in our barracks session I learned to use the throttle. A loop — — — — — — — Nothing to it.

Early on, one day, my instructor was real bitchy — gruff — mean. When we got up, he started doing very violent half snaps — first one way, then the other. A half snap is the beginning of an over the top spin, except you switch the controls and catch the plane in the opposite turn. He was trying to make me air sick — and I didn't — but those turns — snaps — had my head banging on the sides of the cockpit. I didn't speak to him anymore that day — nor he to me.

I got one pink slip from him — three and you were washed out. He set me up, but it was a good lesson. On a check ride he jerked the throttle off and said, "Dead stick landing" — that meant with no power. There was a beautiful field to my left and back — and I turned to make my base leg — I turned downwind — a no no. I always knew where the wind was from after that — from our briefings, or a smoke stack — or something.

He was awful bad about banging your knees with the stick. He rode in the front cockpit. The sticks worked together. All at once — to get our attention — hard jerk the stick sideways — hit a knee on the bone — and hurt like hell. But, he was a good instructor. Everything I didn't learn in the barracks sessions, he taught me. I was good — no bragging.

I loved to fly. It was exciting. A whole other world up there. It was fun. I liked it. I worked at it, for I knew I had to be as good as or better than the pilots I'd meet in combat.

It was warm weather. There was a fence all the way around the field — the gate was in the middle of a one mile leg. We would head out left — turn left at the crossroad — one mile — left at the next crossroad — one mile — and left to the gate — four whole miles. We ran this every day, and a few days twice. We were given 28 min, then 27, then 26 — don't remember where we ended, but, if you didn't do it in the prescribed time, you had to walk a tour — in full uniform — with rifle — 50 min. parading — 10 min. rest. One day I bulled up. I was tired of running. I turned left at the first corner and started walking. Three others joined me. We hitched a ride on a truck with a flat-bed to the next corner. The ones in front were already out of sight on the back leg. No chance for second thoughts — so we walked — left again — and about half way on that leg we started running so we'd work up a sweat. We turned toward the gate at full speed and into the gate — the Lieutenant that checked us in was gone. He thought everyone was already in.

One further note: One of our cadets was killed when he tried to do a roll about 50 feet off the ground.

BASIC TRAINING - ENID, OKLAHOMA

Basic flying training at Enid, Okla., was one of the darker periods of my whole life. Remember that primary training was all but civilian operated. Enid was pure army, and I was a barracks commander. I have wondered many times how I got that job — because of my record in primary? — had attended Clemson? — was tall? — or somebody thought they needed to make a man out of me? Whatever the reason, I took it as punishment. I was totally in charge of about 60 cadets. There were no other cadet officers in the barracks. I was their leader — their nursemaid — had to hear all their gripes — and was responsible for their welfare. I led them, in formation, wherever we had to go. As, I suppose could be expected, there were some smart asses. One of the first things that happened was, we were returning from somewhere — marching up the street beside our barracks. We had to go to the headquarters area to be dismissed. As we passed our barracks, about 10 cadets near the rear broke ranks and ran into the barracks. I kept the formation moving and back stepped until I was sure no one else would break ranks. We were dismissed, and, fortunately, no regular army people noticed we were not a full compliment. I could have been "washed out" of flying training for an act like that. When I got to the barracks, I called an assembly. I didn't raise my voice — but, I was madder than hell. I told them that I didn't know all those that broke ranks, but if it ever happened again, I would take them to the parade ground — the whole outfit — and drill them till their damn tongues hung out. No more breaking ranks.

The worst thing that happened was that when one of my cadets got a gig, I got one too. One gig consisted of marching for 50 minutes — 10 minute rest — in full uniform — white gloves and all — with a rifle — in a quadrangle at headquarters. A sergeant in the main office kept track of your gigs and when they were walked off. Every Saturday morning we had barracks inspection by a Lt., Cap't. or Major — or all three. Each cadet was responsible for his own bed — made up to measurements — locker, and personal appearance — proper haircut, clothes clean, shoes shined — and no dust anywhere. This was where I was getting my gigs. I formed work details to clean the rest of the barracks, and I never got one gig for anything wrong with the building. In fact, the Major said our latrine was the cleanest one he had ever seen — I had that detail to even polish the piping coming to the toilets.

That same morning I was making my last rounds about the barracks and I found a little bit of mud in the hallway just inside the front door. I ran for a rag and was down cleaning up the mud when the door opened, there stood the major — and me down on my hands and knees. I jumped to attention — yelled Atten-ute, and the major, with a studied look, asked who was the barracks commander? "I am sir." He lit in on me and chewed my butt clean off — as only an army major can. The gist of it was that I was the officer in charge — was to supervise and delegate jobs — and if I did my job properly, I wouldn't have time to get down on my knees and scrub a floor. That's much nicer than the way he put it.

Back to gigs — after I had walked 4 or 5 tours, I called an assembly. I opened with, "I have walked my last tour because of some of you damned S.O.B.s. If one of you gets a gig, I'll give you two more (I had the authority) — two gigs and you get four from me. Any questions?" I finished walking the tours I had — but no more gigs.

A flu epidemic hit. The weather was cold. It snowed regularly. We were all miserable. I didn't get the flu, but I got lots of gripes — uniform of the day was sweat shirt and pants in 0 degrees weather for P.T. — had to sit every third seat on movie night, but crowded us together all other times — more and more cadets getting sick from getting their feet wet and frozen at retreat parades — and lots more — and they kept telling me I was in charge and had to do something about it. There was not one major complaint that didn't have merit. I felt the same way. So, I checked how to make a complaint — first line of authority, who was a pissy-assed washed-out lieutenant (heard he was washed out in advanced training for flying under a bridge about 15 feet from the water). Washed-out cadets that went on to officer's school and became Lts. (known as 90 day wonders) and ended up in administration (known as ground pounders) were much more difficult to deal with than regular army officers. I gave a military knock on his door — one rap — and waited — seemed forever. Finally, I heard him say, "Enter." I stood at attention for a long time while he made out like he had very important paperwork to do. I knew better — the S.O.B. Finally, he looked up. "Yes." He did not give me an "At ease." I remained at attention the full time I was there. I said, "Sir," and listed all the complaints. When I was through, he said, "Cadet, you will learn that the army has a reason for everything it does. Dismissed." I about-faced my clenched teeth and departed. I suppose that I was the only barracks commander to face the lion in his den, and conditions improved. Maybe that S.O.B. thought we were going to revolt — or something.

Before I got to Enid my cussing amounted to a few darns, dangs, and dad burns, but it didn't take me long to pick up army cussing. It was effective. It got results.

One really nice thing happened in Enid. One Sunday morning I went into Enid to the Episcopal Church. I got there early and went back to the choir room and asked the organist and choir director, a very wonderful lady, if I might sing with the choir. She said, "Why, sure. Where is your home?" I said, "Asheville, N. C." "Do you by chance know Dr. Arnold Dann?" I told her that I had sung in his choir for several years. She was ecstatic. She said that I would have to sing a solo, which I told her I couldn't do. I was a follower. She was infatuated with Dann — had kept up with him through an Organist Journal — asked me all about him. She apparently thought that anyone that could sing for Arnold Dann could certainly sing solos. Dann was an Englishman, trained by teachers in Dresden and Leipzig, was conductor of the Montreal Symphony, and ended up as organist and choir director at All Souls Episcopal Church in Biltmore, N.C.

After church she asked me to come to Sunday dinner at her home — said it wouldn't be much, but that I was welcome. That was the first home cooked food in forever, and I loved it.

Flying at Enid — and the classes — were all routine, but much more intense than in primary. We flew the BT13 — the Vultee Vibrator we called it.

I was glad to leave Enid.

ADVANCED FLYING TRAINING

FOSTER FIELD
UNIVERSITY OF THE AIR
VICTORIA, TEXAS

What a wonderful place! Any place would have looked good to me after Enid. But this place had an air of elegance. We were treated differently — our instructors were mostly returned combat veterans — tough, but they smiled and had a camaraderie with us. We were almost officers. Most of the goof-ups were already gone. My instructor was Robert Frost from New Hampshire and a veteran of the South Pacific where he flew P-40s and P-39s. Of the cadets assigned to him, he washed one out after his first check ride. That left Prather from Texas, Price from Tennessee, another P — from the South that I can't remember, and me. He couldn't get over us Southern boys — our individuality — our sense of humor — the fact that we were intelligent. He loved to talk to us — ask us question after question — where we grew up — went to school — had we ever travelled north — what size town we grew up in — where did our parents come from — their parents — why did we mistreat the blacks — and, on and on. He said that when he was growing up that he was taught, "If you ever have to go South, don't go anywhere by yourself. Some damned Southerner will shoot you. They're all a bunch of renegades." He was about ten years older than we were, and we were kinda amazed at him — and he at us. Near the end of advanced, he would occasionally invite us over to the officers club for a drink. We'd sit around a table and tell all kinds of tales. He couldn't ask enough questions about Southern girls. One late afternoon he said, "Gentlemen, I've come to a decision. If you damn Southern boys are going to draw a color line, you have to draw it right below Lena Horne."

Boy was he a good pilot! He could really rack an AT-6 around — get everything out of it that it could stand. The AT-6 was a beautiful little plane — wheels retracted — lots more power than we had flown but still limited — low ceiling because it did not have a pressurized carburetor. (The navy called them SNJ-5s). We got in lots of flying time. I looked forward to the next time I could get in one. I became part of that plane, and it part of me. I'd talk to it, "All right, Son, we're going to <u>have</u> a ride today. Get those horses reared up and let's go."

Everyone should learn to fly a plane by themselves. There's no other experience like it to be found on the ground. There's a sense of detachment, of freedom. You become a free spirit. There's a tingling calm — a sense of peace with something you've never known before — something that is vast and unknown — suspended — floating in time. Everything has changed — except you and the plane. As you climb higher and higher, objects on the ground get smaller and smaller until they disappear and become part of other changing patterns of larger areas of forests and fields. Colors constantly change, too. The best example is to be over 10,000 ft. on a clear day, flying to the west in late afternoon. The colors are brilliant. Then turn to an east heading and it is black dark — lights will already be on ahead of you on the ground.

While descending, objects will become more and more familiar, and as you taxi to a stop, cut off the engine, climb to the ground, look skyward, you think, "It's wonderful up there."

The first few days the AT-6 and I became such good friends. We did all the usual turns, stalls (power on and off), spins, and loops. One of my favorite loops was the 4 leaf clover — wasn't that easy, really — took a good bit of precision. Line up with a road below — enter the second loop 90 degrees to the first — and so on — until the last downward leg was back where you began.

One day I said, "OK, Son, we're going to do things I'll bet you haven't done before — well, maybe. Let's see — we'll head down the road and at the top of the loop we'll half roll to straight and level and be headed up the road." Nothing to that. Then we tried to roll out of the upside of a loop and be headed down the road. We never did quite perfect that one. Next, was a hammer head stall — on the upside of a loop we continued straight up — power on — and just before stalling — kick the rudder hard — the nose would fall through straight down (I had enough of flying backwards) and we'd be zizzing at the bottom. We learned to do a four leaf clover using hammer heads. He'd have me sweating sometimes. I didn't always do what he wanted to do, and we'd slide or fall out of a maneuver — climb back up and try to do it together next time. One day, we decided we were going to do a roll on the up leg of a loop — come over the top — do a roll on the down leg — and still be headed down the road. We came close several times but never did hit that road exactly.

On other days when those beautiful, lovely, puffy clouds that south Texas is noted for would be hanging around, one of my bunk buddies and I would make it up to go dog fight. We'd join up after take-off and fly well away from the field — pick out a road below — one would turn in the opposite direction — count — each would — 10 seconds — 1001, 1002, 1003, etc. — then break toward one another head on — and as we passed try to maneuver to get on the other's tail, the other would head toward one of those billowy clouds — skimming the edges — diving underneath — climbing back up and through a saddle — or, as a last resort, fly into a cloud — the other didn't follow — just waited until he came out. While in a cloud I have become disoriented — not knowing up from down — what attitude I was in — whether I was flying in a circle — or what. I would always lose airspeed. When in trouble it's almost impossible not to pull the stick back. Most of the time I would fall out the bottom of the cloud.

I worked at flying. I loved flying. All the stunt flying — finding out what a plane could do and what we could do together — falling out of clouds and all — saved my life in combat.

P.S. The only maneuver I never tried was an outside loop. Thought about it a lot. I never heard of anyone doing one in an AT-6.

I learned to fly on instruments in a link trainer. It was a machine in a classroom that was like a cockpit of an airplane. I'd climb in — a sergeant would close the lid — the instrument panel was lit up — all the instruments were there — air speed, altimeter, flight indicator, rate of climb indicator, a gyro and magnetic compass, and needle and ball. The hardest thing to learn — after jerking an airplane around — was not to tilt the gyro. It tilted — tumbled at 60 degrees. After I became proficient in the link, I did the same thing in an airplane with a hood pulled down so I couldn't see out. I became a qualified instrument pilot — with license and all.

Next, was cross-country — both day and night — filed our own flight plan — distances — time between — windage — and headings. Daytime was a snap. Night flying could become a little hairy. The wind most always blew from the gulf inland during the day and from inland to the gulf at night. Our last leg was always downwind, and it was very easy to overshoot the field. We heard that there were cadets that landed in the gulf because they ran out of fuel.

All classes were over — we flew 12 hours and off 12 hours. At 12:01 p.m. every other day, three of us would go fight "The Battle of Houston." Little Tommy Reeves had been a trumpet man in Woody Herman's orchestra — Jones, who had "big blue," a Buick, had had his own orchestra in Oklahoma

City. They both had girls in Houston. Jones found out that I knew a little bit about music — had me sing a whole tone scale — said his girl, Puddin, had a friend that needed a date and would I go with them? I sure didn't take time to think about it. "Sure will."

We went to Puddin's house. Her father was a bank president. Their house was awesome — unbelievable. The foyer was all marble with a beautiful chandelier — to the left two steps down into the living room with 16 ft. high ceiling and blue velvet drapes over the windows from ceiling to floor. To the right was first a card room with at least 20 tables — then a large library — then, a music room with two grand pianos, then, a large sun room. Out back were tennis courts, large swimming pool, and an 18-hole golf course — some estate!

The girls would have eats — hot dogs or something — and beer. We'd go to a park on a lake and spend most of our time. One evening we came home and Puddin had forgotten her key — so we piled back in the car, and it seemed forever while we drove to the backdoor. We all went in the kitchen, and there sat Puddin's mother in a beautiful dressing gown with her boyfriend who graciously excused himself. Mother gave each (man) of us a pinch bottle of Scotch before we left.

P.S. Tommy is the only person I ever saw smoke Marijuana. I tried it one time and didn't feel a thing.

I graduated from flying school — was commissioned a 2nd Lt. — and got a 14-day delay en route from Foster Field to Foster Field — I headed home.

It seemed that the training had gone on forever. I had come a long way — a long rough way. I had made it. I was a pilot — an officer. I was proud — proud of myself — proud for my parents — and my friends. I wore my greens — packed my pinks in my B4 bag (no more duffle bags) — took the stiffener out of the top of my cap — so it would slouch over properly — and headed home.

The only thing I now remember, while there, was meeting Eleanor. My Aunt Marylee introduced us. I was stunned when I saw Eleanor — she was the most beautiful 19-year-old girl I ever saw. She captured my heart — her smile — her glistening eyes — the way she walked — her warmth — she was super-intelligent — and besides, she had a figure that made my eyes bug out.

I remembered what Aunt Lindy said about Uncle Gus, my Great-grandparents that lived way back in the mountains of Madison county — "The first time I ever laid eyes on Eleanor, I knowed she was my woman."

Two major events of my whole life happened in less than a week — becoming a pilot — and meeting the most wonderful person in the whole world.

Back at Foster Field our class of pilots were split in half — gunnery training on Matagorda Island, and transition flying in a P-40 "Warhawk." I was in the P-40 half. The P-40 had been the workhorse fighter plane in the Pacific and North Africa. It was being replaced by P-47s and P-51s. It had a long nose out in front of you with an inline liquid cooled engine. The cockpit was small. In fact, the seat was all the way down on the floor, causing the pilot to sit with his legs straight out in front of him to reach the rudder pedals. The stick was very short — no more than 16" long. The most fascinating thing was the gun sight — ring and pin — both out on the cowling — the ring near the windshield, and the pin out toward the engine. When we got into the war that is all that pilots had to shoot by.

Then to Matagorda Island for aerial and ground gunnery in AT-6s. The AT-6 felt good again. I was a hot pilot, as I have said before. We were one. We knew each other. We could do anything — well, almost. My friend taught me a lesson. We had a small, short runway, and there was always a crosswind on take-offs and landings. On this particular landing we were too high on our last turn — had about a 45 degree strong crosswind — and I said, "Son, we'll just slip you down a few feet." I crossed controls — right rudder, left stick — had practiced and done this lots of times. All at once that damned plane quit flying — we were exactly 90 degrees to the crosswind. We fell like a ton of bricks. I pushed the throttle wide open — corrected the controls, and just as we got straight, we hit the runway. We bounced back into the air. I don't know how the landing gear withstood such a jolt. It was awful. With the throttle wide open and not enough runway left to land, we went around — made a good approach — and landed the way I should have the first time. That's the last time I was ever a hot pilot. From then on I could never fly quite good enough to suit me — close, but not quite. I felt like that AT-6 was laughing at me, "I showed you something different, didn't I?" — — — — — — No one ever said a word. An officer has privileges — the privilege of making an ass out of himself — or killing himself — or both.

Ground gunnery was a snap. I grew up shooting a gun. Now, the gun wasn't to my shoulder — I was sitting between them. We fired at targets mounted on frames that were tilted back a little bit. I knew I was scoring well because I could see dust boiling up behind the target. Aerial gunnery was different.

A twin engine plane pulled a target made out of screen wire fastened to iron rods weighted at the bottom to hold the wire vertical. The wire was about 4 ft. by 30 ft. The ammunition — the bullet part — was dipped in paint — blue — yellow — red — and if you got a hit you could tell by the color on the wire. The tow plane would let the target out on a cable about 200 ft. behind him. As he flew up and down the coast, each of us 4 would get a chance to intercept him — always going in from the side and shooting deflection shots — always shooting out over the gulf. When all the ammunition was fired, we would return to the field. He would fly over slowly and low and drop the target, which was picked up and spread on a long table. We could count our hits ourselves. Once in a while a target would come in with long slits in it — up to 6". That meant the pilot firing was coming awfully close to hitting the tow ship.

RICHMOND ARMY AIR FORCE BASE

Back at Foster Field after gunnery training, we were put on a troop train with Pullman cars — what luxury — headed for Richmond Army Air Force Base — now, Byrd Field. We had barely started moving when a crap (dice) game opened up in one of the cars. There was a blond-headed fellow that took all the gambling money on the train — even the Pullman porter's railroad pocket watch. He wired home money in Memphis and Knoxville — at least $500.00 a stop.

When the train stopped in Knoxville for servicing, I jumped off as quick as I could and found Jim Clodfelter, a supervisor that had once been my daddy's boss in Asheville. He let me in his office, and I cranked the phone — still had grapevine phones then — and got through to my dad. Was he surprised! We talked for quite a while — in between others coming in on the line to take care of business.

Richmond was great. We flew transition in P-47s. What an aeroplane! Even with the RPM redlined and low octane gasoline it was a dream to fly. Each instructor had 5 pilots to look after except the C.0. — he had two — Price and me. He was a Cap't. and a West Point grad and rougher than a cob — but fair.

The first chance he got he took us for a check ride — Price on his right wing — I was on his left. He sent Price out a little ways and had him go through several maneuvers — called him back — told me to space myself and do a half roll. When I turned that baby upside down, gallons of gasoline poured into the cockpit with me. The canopy was full. I slid out of that roll violently, losing several thousand feet. I watched the gasoline drain through the metal floor and disappear. I didn't touch anything electrical. I moved the oxygen to pure oxygen — sat there — it was quiet. I finally slid my canopy back a notch — mechanically, I hadn't even thought of the C.O. Finally, when I figured the gas had evaporated and the fumes dissipated, I mashed the radio button — electric — and called him — nothing — no sound. Our radio had two hookups — one to the mike in the oxygen mask, and one to the earphones — the earphones were unplugged. When I slid out my head went to one side and jerked the plug out. I plugged in — could hear again. The C.O. was hotter than a blue barreled pistol. I told him I had gasoline in the cockpit. "All right," he said, "Let's go home," in a real mean voice. We were at 20,000 feet. He literally dived at the field. We were going so fast that we had to circle the field twice to slow down enough for the traffic pattern. When I taxied to stop he was on my wing. "Lt. did you say you had gas fumes in your cockpit," with lots of sarcasm. I said, "No sir, I had gasoline." His manner changed immediately. He was stunned. He knew he was looking at a miracle. My chances had been slim to none. He jumped down — walked about six steps — turned and said, "Ponder, you take my plane, and you and Price go back up and practice awhile."

About 2-½ hours later when I climbed out of the C.O.'s plane, I saw the crew chief sitting all hunched over in the cockpit of my plane. I went over — climbed onto the wing and asked the sergeant what he found. He said he had never been through anything like this before. He said <u>that man</u> had chewed them all to pieces. After going over the plane with a fine tooth comb they reported to the C.O. that they didn't find anything. He said the C.O. exploded. "I know there was gasoline in that cockpit. Get everyone on the flight line on that plane. Dismantle that damned plane to the ground, if you have to — but find it. Is that clear?" "We found it," the sergeant said. The engine had just been through major maintenance, and the 4-inch return line to the top of the main tank had not been fastened back. He looked up at me with a troubled face, "Lt., you sure are lucky."

I knew he was right. I knew that fumes from gasoline were much more explosive than dynamite. One little teensy-tiny electrical spark and that's "all she wrote." It happened a few days later. A general had come to RAAFB to see his son — a well-built black-headed boy. The Gen. was standing on the flight line waiting for the boy to land. As the boy made his last turn from the base leg, his plane all but disintegrated. Gas fumes exploding was the <u>only</u> explanation. A hell of a thing for a father to watch.

At night, all the east coast was blacked out — or supposed to be. About 20 miles northeast of our field there was a duplicate camouflaged field. A few lights were left on there to silhouette buildings or whatever. I never saw a better decoy.

The first night landing I shot was something else. The only light on the whole field was a search light — probably 10 feet in diameter — mounted on the back of a truck which was parked to one side near the end of the runway. The light was directed down the runway. I came in with a nice easy approach — broke my glide — pulled the throttle — and kabloomie — I had landed in the top of the light beam and dropped from there to the runway.

I bounced — did I ever — shoved the throttle wide open and walked the plane back to the runway. I was moving on — fast — hotter than a pistol. We had good long runways or I would have gone around — a lot of the boys did. It was rather comical to watch. All those planes bouncing — engine revving up. We learned to fly down into the light to reach the runway. (Walking a plane down is a good description. Nose high — throttle on. To keep lined up with the runway it's necessary to shove the rudder pedals first one way then the other. Sometimes the tail wheel hits the runway first).

One night that was pitch black we flew a group flight in flights of four — an instructor and three more. The instructor took off and climbed to the left. I did likewise and tried to pick up his tail light — I saw it — it was moving. I began having trouble keeping my air speed up. I kept my eye on that tail light — it wasn't moving any more — it was a damned star. I looked farther left and picked him up. He had me join on his right — ease in — down a little — back a little, in a little more — hold it right there. I couldn't see his plane. All I could see was his right wingtip light — the fiery exhaust from the engine — and his taillight — this made a triangle. I kept that exact triangle for about the next three hours. We kept making turns until 48 planes were all in one formation. The next turn was Washington, D.C. I caught a glimpse of the plane from reflection of lights as we turned at Roanoke, Va. Our last turn was at Roanoke Rapids, N.C. — then home.

When we weren't flying, our time was our own. One Sunday morning I went to the Episcopal Church downtown. A group of older ladies made sure all visitors got a tour and history of the church — where Robert E. Lee, etc. sat, and when. Bless their hearts; they were still fighting the Civil War.

I ate a few times at a restaurant up the street from the John Marshall Hotel. Had pictures hanging on the wall of all the celebrities that had eaten there. The food was really good. My favorite was crab meat sautéed in butter.

Southern hospitality? A group of girls from the Richmond Country Club invited us out to a dance. I met a good looking tall girl that invited me back to play tennis and have dinner. I thought I was a pretty good tennis player, but she beat my socks off. There was no food rationing at that place. The long tables were bending in the middle — and was it good.

NORFOLK, VIRGINIA

Our next move was to Norfolk, Va., for gunnery in P-47s. We fired at ground targets near Langley Field and out over the Atlantic at tow targets. We flew off of a civilian field — we used one runway and civilian aircraft the other. There were two one story barracks with screened-in porches for officers stationed there. The rest of us stayed in Quonset huts. There were boardwalks from each to the latrine and shower and mess hall that were in the middle of the complex.

One Sunday we had chicken a la king for lunch. That afternoon Capt. Jack, (last name), a doctor, went by the kitchen to see what was for supper — same chicken a la king. He asked if it shouldn't be refrigerated. No sir, we're keeping it hot enough. Next morning I was near the latrine, and I heard this pitiful yell, "I can't make it, I can't make it, I can't make it." He burst out of his door onto the screen porch, banged the screen door open, down the steps, tried to run on the boardwalk, got about halfway to the latrine, finally gave up, jumped over into the sand, pulled his shorts down — all he had on — and let go. He had the G.I.'s. From what I heard, he demoted everybody in the kitchen that day.

Out on the flight line that morning we had our parachutes strapped on ready to leave the briefing room. Lt. Brown, one of my good buddies, came to the door and motioned for me. I stepped outside, thinking he wanted to tell me something. I broke his fall as he passed out. He, too, had the G.I.s — filled his flight suit full.

The officer in charge was pretty smart. He asked how many of us ate in the mess hall the night before — about half had not. "You men are grounded until the flight surgeon ok's you," he said. Since I couldn't fly, I rode in the ambulance with Brown to a hospital at Virginia Beach. I stayed with him a little while after they got him in a room. That's the last time I ever saw him. Our paths never crossed again.

At our first briefing the C.O. stood up and said, "Take a good look at me." He had flown P-40s in the Pacific. Much of his face and hands were scar tissue — not pretty to look at. "This was caused by a flash explosion. I'm giving each one of you here an order. If you smell gas fumes in your cockpit, bail out." I dropped my head because I had to grin. He didn't mention raw gas and fumes.

Herman and Pearl Jarvis — two very wonderful people. Pearl had worked at the Bon Marche in Asheville with my Aunt Leona. Then she moonlighted in the evening at the ticket booth at the Plaza Theater. Herman was an officer in the Asheville fire department, and when I went there to see my Uncle Hubert, Leona's husband, Herman would come walking up — shake my hand — and we'd sit on a bench. We had several long talks about everything.

Herman was now a captain on a fireboat in the harbor. They lived in a two-story duplex. When I learned that I was going to Norfolk, I got their address and phone number from home. I phoned. Herman answered, "You got to come over. Can't wait to see you" — and on. We fixed our schedules — decided the day — at 6:00 p.m. Home. I was going home. They were home-folks. I had never been in their home in Asheville, but here I was "going home." We were more than friends — we loved one another.

I went in, and Herman said, "Let's go. We're having seafood. We're going down to the fishing dock. What do you want to eat?" We decided on steamed crabs. You could tell Herman was a regular customer. This fellow grinned real big when Herman told him that I was from the mountains — had never eaten a crab — wanted a dozen of the largest he had; He put the crabs in a metal pot — put the lid on — and hit them with live steam for a short time. With tongs, he filled a brown peck bag full — picked up a shaker of cayenne pepper and shook and shook on the crabs.

On the way home Herman said that Pearl was working at ship's service 'till 9:00 p.m., but that she had baked us a pone of cornbread. After a drink — we both liked bourbon — we pitched in. Herman taught me how to crack the meat out. Every so often, we'd get up and go to the kitchen sink and wash our hands and mouth. "Zee red pepper was hotter than hell."

That fellow at the dock had put 20 crabs in that bag. Pearl came in about that time and we both hugged her — for her — and then for her cornbread. I felt like a dog. We had left her a smidgen of cornbread and 4 crabs.

Two other things happened at Norfolk in my flying:

There was a free French squadron on the field going through the same training as I was. They didn't speak English but did have their own air wave frequency with the tower. I had just landed and was less than half way down the runway when I heard this gosh awful noise. This Frenchman was landing almost right behind me. The tower apparently told him to pull up and go around. He passed over my left wing with his engine wide open and his wheels just barely missed. As I was slowing near the end of the runway, my air controller said, "Whew!" "Close!"

The other thing was a freak — a mechanical no-no. When we parked a P-47 we locked all the control surfaces in neutral and the tail wheel which had its own lock. There was a spring-loaded locking mechanism at the bottom and in front of the stick. To unlock the stick and rudder pedals you put your finger under a lever type handle — not very large — and pull up and a spring would snap it forward. I did all this, I thought. My stick was unlocked and free. The rudder pedals felt OK, but the locking spring overtook the forward spring and had my rudder pedals in locked position. Most all taxiing was done with brake pedals. I got lined up on the runway — locked my tail wheel straight — gunned my engine — blew my tail up — I started trying to veer left — pushed my right rudder pedal hard — finally had to use right brake — jabs of it — to stay on the runway. Finally, I was airborne. I controlled my direction with the ailerons and elevators. When I got to altitude and straight and level at about 250 mph, I had no problem. I checked the rudder pedals and they would move just so far. I figured a rudder cable was jammed with something — maybe slipped out of a pulley wheel. I went on with my flight — fired at two targets — got 4 hits — most of anyone. By the time I was ready to land I had it figured out — go in with right wing low — hit right wheel first — when the plane settled to the runway — hit the right brake — hit it — hit it — tromp down on it. When I parked, I reached down to lock the controls. That damned lock was in locked position. I had a flash of rage. I sat back in the seat — took a real deep breath and motioned for the crew chief. I had him lean over to where he could see. Almost every time I tried the lock, the locking spring jerked it back into locked position. I said, "Sergeant, that thing nearly got me killed."

That experience very probably saved my life later on. The more I flew, the more philosophical I became. It was like I was being tested — like, pay attention — there are things you don't know yet. The idea that a plane could fly without all of its controls never entered my mind — but it will!

From the day, back in Texas, when I quit being a hot pilot, I flew in earnest — with patience — with calmness. That's when I really began to learn to fly.

Transition training in the P-47 was nearly over. At first it felt big and kinda clumsy. That was my fault. We began to make friends. She became more beautiful every time I got in one. She was heavy — built like a bumble bee — solid — no vibrations — weighed about 5 tons — later with armament — 7 tons on a little 41 ft. wingspread. The P-47 was designed and built by Republic Aviation as a high altitude fighter. The P-51 Mustang was designed as a medium attack fighter. In combat we were swapped — the P-51 up — and the P-47 down. The P-51 had an inline liquid-cooled Allison engine, and the tubing in the cooling system ran to a coil on the belly of the fuselage and behind the cockpit, one little hole anywhere in the system about the size of a pencil eraser and the engine would overheat and stick within two minutes. The P-47 with its radial air-cooled engine could take an untold amount of damage and still fly.

While at Richmond I took her to altitude 30,000 ft., her top ceiling was 42,000. Cruising speed at 30,000 ft. was 425 mph, and controls were so responsive that it seemed you didn't move them, all you had to do was think, and the plane would respond. What a dream to fly!

Another significant difference — in a dive the P-51 was redlined at 7.9 G's. More than that and the wings might fold up. The "G" pull of the P-47 was unlimited. The pilot would black out long before there was any danger to the plane.

From about 6 miles up one could begin seeing the curvature of the earth. Down below, things were a lot different — roads and railroads mostly disappeared — areas took on larger proportions. It was like looking at something that wasn't there. You knew it was — but it wasn't. The sky — what was on the ground — the feeling of flying — all took on different dimensions.

The engine in that baby doll was an eighteen cylinder, twin bank, air-cooled, (9 cylinders to the bank) made by Pratt and Whitney. What a beautiful piece of engineering. In its day — in its time — there was no better. It turned a four blade propeller — all the other engines had no more than three. I have always wondered — which came first — the engine or the plane? P&W engines were used in other planes, but how Republic and P&W got together — and kept improving the P-47 — is somewhat of a miracle. The last '47 I flew had a P&W R-2800 engine — 2800 indicating horse power. Actual HP was probably around 2500 to 2600. Just imagine sitting right behind and controlling something that powerful. One day I fantasized how I'd hook up that many live horses to the nose of the plane — one line straight ahead

— or 10 abreast in a block. I chose a pyramid so I'd have a lead horse. Near the end of the war P&W built an 11-3000 engine. That didn't work out. They were tested on some '47s in England and were so powerful that they twisted off the motor mounts.

OVERSEAS

Training in this country was over. It had taken a year, almost. The government had spent about $20,000 getting me ready for combat. I had a good record — had learned lots — had coped in situations that had been dangerous. I was going to do the very best I could.

Back to Richmond, where we were issued winter clothing and shoes — canteen and mess kit — and a 45 caliber pistol. I had never shot a pistol of any kind but a few times. This 45 was heavy and cumbersome and tried to jump up out of your hand when fired. In fact, when I qualified as expert, I bounced two bullets off the ground up through the target.

We all got our booster shots — in both arms again. And oh! That dentist. I didn't have a filling in my head, and he said I had to have two fillings. I said he was crazy as hell, but he said I had two little spots — preventive dentistry — he said. I argued, he won.

We went from Richmond to Camp Kilmer, N.J., a transient point. We left Kilmer in buses to a dock in

NYC. We boarded the Aquitania — a British ship. That's not exactly true. The Aquitania and two sister ships — the Mauretania, and I think, maybe the Lusitania, were taken from the Germans at the end of WWI as war reparations. [Actually, the Lusitania, a British ocean liner, was sunk by a German submarine in 1915.]

We sailed — went through all kinds of drills — learned our station in case we had to abandon ship. We were crowded with all kinds of troops. We were alone — no convoy. We were fast enough to outrun the German subs.

The British crew let the word out that they were interested in taking on any American on board in the art of fisticuffs — for money of course. The third day out as many as could gathered on one of the top decks. There were 10 bouts, and the boxers were matched by weight, and gloves were used. The heavyweight bout was something to see. The American was a bull — big — heavy — and mean. He charged that Britisher time after time. The Briton kept his gloves up — his elbows in close — and cut the American to pieces. Blood was everywhere.

The Americans didn't win a bout.

The officer's mess was something else. The British really respect officers. We sat at tables — with tablecloths and were served courses. One was a fish course served in a small soup bowl, a different fish every night — cod, haddock, don't remember the other two.

SHREWSBURY

The ship slowed, and sometime after dark we docked in Glasgow. There were no lights anywhere. We were one of the first units off — carried our B-4 and duffle bag to a waiting train — and were on our way south — to Shrewsbury, where we spent a week flying souped-up '47s — high octane (150) gas and more powerful engines that could be run wide open (engines had been redlined at about 2200 rpm back in the states as I remember).

What a horse I was flying now. I hadn't anticipated anything so beautiful — the power — the maneuver-ability — just absolutely fabulous.

Then one day I climbed to altitude above the clouds and was just sitting there, when all at once a thought hit me, "What in the hell am I doing here?" All I had ever done since I was a little boy was go to school or train for something. I'd finished high school, Jr. College, trained as an apprentice on the railroad, and trained as a pilot. I hadn't lived. I hadn't been out in the world. There were so many experiences I hadn't done but looked forward to. Was I now going to be shortchanged?

Then I knew. I knew what had to be. I knew those efficient, mechanical-minded Germans were going to do their best to kill me. I knew I had one chance — to kill them first.

In a few minutes I made peace with myself. All the unknown anxieties were gone. I had a job to do, and, damn it to hell, I'd be the best exterminator in Europe.

That same day a little smart-alecked kind of boy that slept in the cot on my left was killed. He failed to pull out of a dive. They said his engine was 8 feet in the ground, and that about 40lbs. of his body was under the engine. Puzzle! I don't know.

The adjutant got his personal belongings. We divided the rest. I got a blanket and his flight boots — small enough for bedroom slippers and were fleece lined.

Shrewsbury is where I met C. J. Mayer, M. E. Johns, Hugh Miller, and Stuart Wilde. One night Mayer and I walked into town, which was black dark. We bumped into a lady that had a little portable cooker and was selling fish and chips. She rolled a piece of newspaper into a cone — put in the potatoes — then the fish on top. Absolutely delicious.

ASSIGNMENT TO A COMBAT UNIT

We were ready. Had everything we owned with us. A C-47 transport landed. We climbed aboard and landed in Paris. A truck picked us up and took us to the "Chateau De Rothschild," a pilot replacement point. Would Bois Boulogne be right? The grounds were encircled by a high rock wall with a wrought iron gate at the entrance. The Germans had mined the whole place. In the daytime German prisoners were used to sap mines on each side of the driveway. At night there were snipers across the road in some woods that would fire at the MP's on the gate. The MP's would answer with their tommy guns, if they thought they heard something. There were about 15 pyramidal tents on what would have been the lawn in front of the house. We slept there. Each tent had a potbellied stove, and the first night a pilot took the lid off to put more coal in. His goon-ball buddy stepped on the lid barefooted. Someone broke open his emergency kit and gave him a shot of morphine; we all went back to sleep.

The captain in charge finally sent for us. I had told Mayer, Johns, Miller, and Wilde that I had an uncle, Warren Trantham, in the 405th fighter group, and I was going there, if possible. That's where we'll go, they said. The 405th needed nine pilots — 5 to the 510th squad, 2 to 509, 2 to 511. The captain said, "I think I ought to tell you, the 405th has one of the largest turnover rates of any P-47 group. You five still want to go? Done."

Each day when the captain got all his info, and nothing was going to happen, he'd tell us we were free until the next morning. We were only there for 3 or 4 days. The first chance we got, Mayer and I took off for Paris. We walked about 3/4 of a mile to the end of the metro line and took the subway into town — did a lot of sightseeing — ended up in the Place De Opera. This was, apparently, the main hub of the Metro. There were at least three lines that crossed here — all at different levels — the bottom level was way down. It was now dark. The square was almost deserted. The buildings, in the blackout, took on eerie looking shapes. Mayer and I found the steps down to the metro. We knew the color line we wanted — found it on the big board chart — went down a level — decided that the lit sign "Sorti" was the way — entered a tunnel and walked and walked. Twice, we started to turn back. No, we'll go ahead. We finally came to some steps — climbed to the sidewalk on a street that was dark as pitch. No sounds. No nothing. Mayer wanted to go right. With my sense of direction I said it had to be left. We were getting close to the time of the last subway out on our line. We went left — walked a long way — heard some voices — we were back to "The Opera." Down the steps we went — found our line — and made the last ride. With all my French in school, I had missed the word Sorti-Exit. Did I ever feel dumb.

When we climbed out to the street at the end of the line, we found our street sign — it took awhile — and started walking. A fog had settled in and it was so dark we couldn't see each other. We heard something. Stopped. Listened. Heard movement in the woods. We pulled our 45's — moved off the sidewalk to the middle of the street. Slowly, carefully, cautiously, we began to walk — holding our pistols straight out in front. After several steps we decided that the fog was so heavy that it was dripping off the trees and hitting the underbrush. On ahead we heard the MP's tommy gun go Brrrrp — holstered our pistols — and walked briskly to the gate.

405th GROUP –
510th FIGHTER SQUADRON

We were flown to St. Dizier, France. On a map St. Dizier made a triangle with Metz and Nancy. The five of us were taken to operations in the 510th compound. We turned in our records, and then were taken to the living area. We said, if possible, we would like to live together. No problem. The fourth tent down on the left is empty.

Someone had really built a fine home. They had found some 4ft. wide fabricated insulation that enclosed all the sides of the tent. They found some concrete blocks to put under the tent pole — just high enough until the tent sides overlapped the insulation on the sides. We could stand up inside the tent. There was a potbellied stove in front of the tent poles with stove pipe extending through the top of the tent. There were six canvas folding cots. Miller took the one on the left side of the door — I, the left wall — Mayer, the back — then Wilde and Johns on the right side.

The first thing I did was make up my bed. I pulled the cot out from the wall — hung my mess kit and canteen on some nails in the wall — and unpacked my blankets. I had three already now. There were two more army blankets on the cot — total of five. I covered the cot with the first blanket with the rest of the blanket on the floor on the right side. The second blanket on the left side — third right — fourth left — fifth right. Then, I folded each blanket to the other side of the cot. I made a bed roll. At the bottom I folded the blankets under to keep my feet from sticking out.

Each night I would fold my lined flying jacket wrong side out and use it for a pillow. I'd take my 45 out of the holster and put it just under the jacket on the right side (there were infiltrators and sympathizers still around). I'd take off my clothes — hang them on nails on the wall — and burrow down into my bedroll. The winter of '44-'45 was one of the coldest on record in Europe. The first time I woke up with snow on my eyelashes gave me a start. But, I was warm. I was in a tent and sleeping on a cot. I wondered how in the hell all those boys up in the front lines that had to sleep on the ground — in pure misery — could survive — not from enemy fire — but the damned cold itself.

COL. RALPH JENKINS

When I came to the 510th our CO was Maj. Ralph Jenkins. Most of the old pilots that started in Walterboro, S.C. were gone — killed in action — prisoner of war — or rotated back to the states. Their leader was still there. Jenks had instilled in each of them that flying together as a squadron they were a fighting force second to none. Whatever the mission might be each pilot did his best as if this was the only mission he might fly.

Each new pilot — and there were many — immediately sensed — got caught up in — the character of the squadron. They quickly learned from the older pilots what was expected of them. All of us were proud to be a part of the best squadron in Europe, Jenks set the pattern and we followed. To me he was a hero.

MY FIRST MISSION

The flight board was the center of attention of each pilot that walked into the ready room — was your name there? Yes. What flight? Red flight. I was flying Capt. Knisley's wing. He was the squadron leader on this mission. Knisley was from near Kingsport, TN. He was an old South Pacific veteran with more combat time than I had flying time. He was a wheelhorse — not afraid of the devil himself. I felt lucky to draw him.

Capt. Pete Harings, intelligence officer, called the twelve of us into his briefing room. On the wall opposite to the door was a big map — probably 8x12 feet — that had a plastic covering over it — with three colored lines zigzagging across it. The top line was green. He said that even though his information was always delayed that it was very doubtful that any of our troops had reached this far. The middle line was yellow. He said that positive identification had to be made before any dive bombing or strafing could be done. The area was fluid and our troops could be anywhere. The red line was on the bottom — our troops. To the left of the big map was a much smaller scale map spotted and blobbed with red dots. Each red dot — smaller than a pin head — was a gun emplacement — three 88 millimeter cannons fired from a center doughnut — we called them — at the same time. 88's. They were heavy flak [abbreviation of Fliegerabwehrkanone] anti-aircraft, fused from 6000 ft. to 30,000 ft. and up. The 88 was the finest, most accurate, most versatile gun used (made) in WWII. It was more like a rifle than a cannon. The red dots that indicated the placement of the 88's were not as big a threat to us as the medium and light flak that protected them. 6,000 feet was kinda the top of the medium and light (meaning smaller caliber) and the bottom of the 88's — except with a deflection shot or with proximity fuses. Going to our target and back home and depending on the weather, we flew as close to 6,000 ft. as possible. There was still lots of flak at times, but we didn't seem to get hit as often.

Each squadron was assigned 25 P-47's. With those that were shot down, and others damaged, most missions were with 12 ships — occasionally 16. Today it was 12 — 3 flights. Each flight had a radio identification color — Red, White, and Blue. Knisley was Red 1. I was Red 2. The element leader was Red 3 and his wingman Red 4 — and so on. Our squadron call name was Jampit.

I drew an older 47 — a razorback — a ridge on top
of the fuselage starting right behind the cockpit
and feathering out farther back. Knisley had the

newest model — P-47 D — with a bubble canopy — no ridge. Capt. Harings gave us a target — the coordinates which I saw Knisley put on his map (air chart). We were to dive bomb an ammunition storage area in Saarbrueken and strafe trains, tanks, vehicles, gun positions, buildings, personnel, and anything else that might be promising — and remember everything you can for debriefing.

And last he said that if we were shot down to make every effort to not get caught — each one of us had an escape kit that could get us by for about a week. It was a sealed plastic container about 6"x 6" x 1" thick and contained concentrated bits of food (cubes), a razor, a map, and German money. If we were taken prisoner, we were to try to escape at every opportunity. This he said would take more Germans to guard us — thus less Germans in a fighting outfit. Also, we were not to give our parole (word) that we wouldn't try to escape except for a limited time — to help another prisoner to the doctor or hospital, or such.

Knisley said for us to put our radio on channel C (common channel) and after we were airborne to switch to channel B — let's go.

We climbed into a couple of jeeps with trailers behind to go to the flight line. I walked up to my ship. The crew chief said she was kinda of a gas hog and to be careful. I climbed up into the cockpit — fastened my safety belt and shoulder straps. The straps were spring loaded and had to be tight enough so you couldn't hit your head on the optical gun sight mounted just a few inches away — maybe 18 inches.

I did my cockpit check and looked out to see I was clear. The crew chief was still standing under the cockpit with his hand on the wing. He yelled, "Good luck," and backed away. I raised my left hand to my head in acknowledgement.

I moved out onto the taxi strip behind Knisley. We eased our way to the marshaling area — turned our tails to the side — checked both magnetos — got clearance from the tower — moved to the runway — spaced myself across from Knisley (took off two ships at a time) — locked my tail wheel — got a nod from Knisley — opened the throttle — moved down the runway that was getting shorter and shorter. I was flying speed and still on the ground. I finally felt the shocks on the wheel struts bounce a little bit — not much runway left. I literally pulled that bastard into the air — immediately lifted the lever to raise the wheels. We were still going straight ahead — still close to the ground. Finally, the wheels were up — airspeed increased — I raised my flaps and followed

Knisley in a climbing turn around the field to form up the squadron.

When two ships were about half way down the runway, two more began their takeoff. By the time that Knisley and I were parallel to the runway all ships were airborne.

I now knew that I was flying a monster. The '47 was heavy, and with 3 500 pound GP bombs — under the belly and each wing — over 400 rounds of 50 caliber ammo in 8 50 caliber machine guns and 625 gallons of gasoline — about 14,000 1bs. — 7 tons on a 41 ft. wingspread, there's no way that a fighter plane can get off the ground with that much weight. No wonder I had felt glued to the runway. While going down that runway and knowing the '47 had done it before, or at least must have, there was some doubt in my faith that it would again.

"Jampit Red 2, Jampit Red 1. Do you read me"? Knisley said. "Roger, Red 1 over and out." I replied. After about 10 minutes Knisley said, "Watch that fortress at Metz. It's still loaded." Patton had surrounded and then bypassed Metz. The Germans were dug in — armed to the teeth — and itching for something to shoot at.

Before I knew it, we were at the front lines. Knisley told the squadron that one of our armored outfits was directly below us and to take a good look. He said, "Blue flight, you stay up for top cover while we make our run." I could see him looking ahead and then studying his map. Then, he started making swooping descending turns — I later learned — for flak evasion. All at once his left wing came up and down he went — almost straight down. By the time I could react, I wasn't far behind. I didn't recognize anything from our briefing. The Germans had waited until we were in our dive before opening up. The whole ground seemed to light up — all over and in patches. Knisley's bombs were away. I tried to hit where he did. At the bottom of the dive — one quick glance backward — I had come close to his. I was low — seemed almost on the ground. With full throttle I wracked that baby to the left to climb inside Knisley and got on his wing again. Knisley — "White flight — we missed — try more to the right." We watched White flight go into their dive from a different angle to ours. The whole sky filled with flak — some bursts were white — others black. There were clouds of flak — so thick that we lost sight of the planes diving through it. We were now at about 4,000 feet. Blue flight had eased in to the area and was making their run at a different angle. No major explosions — just the bombs.

As soon as Blue flight's bombs exploded, Knisley headed in. Down we went — almost to the ground. He picked out some trucks. I was on his right wing jockeying my throttle to keep from getting ahead of him. When he fired — I fired next — about 3 second bursts — flak was popping all around and in front of us — the road, trucks, buildings started sparkling. We were firing API — armor piercing incendiary bullets. Knisley turned to the left — I followed. All at once there was a complete wall of fire right in front of us. The only time in 51 missions that I saw anything like it. We were headed right into it. I was stunned. My lips grew tight. I sucked breath between my teeth. My eyes seemed to pop. I was climbing right into it, the '47 felt like it quit flying — like I was suspended and couldn't move. The damn flak was all around me. My instincts took over. From the climbing turn to the left I jerked the stick back — hit the right rudder hard — half snapped into a dive to the right — straight into the wall — picked up speed — wracked us to the left — back to the right — pulled up sharply to the left and came up on the outside of Knisley. I was shocked. I hadn't been hit. It wasn't my time. Impossible — no way even a wren could have survived that. I was limp — exhausted — thankful — mad as hell — those Germans were playing for keeps — damn their souls. I knew it ahead of time, but didn't expect anything like this. I felt sick inside. My inner being was on hold. If it was going to be like this, there was no way I could survive.

Lord! Here we go again. Knisley broke down — we went in low — hit some more trucks — but he didn't pull up. We were on the building tops — he stayed there. We finally broke to the left — we were out of their range — we climbed and went back in until we began to fire tracers — that meant we had 50 rounds per gun left. Knisley and I headed back home. The squadron was scattered. It was kinda like each man was on his own — doing his job — destroying all that he could — and head home — listening to the sweet hum of the engine.

We were passing Metz. I saw the element — Red 3 & 4 back on the left. Closing and farther back were the other two flights. Knisley, "Jampit — anybody take flak?" "Roger, Jampit — Red 4 in the wing, out." "Jampit 1 — White 3 out." Red 1, "OK to land?" "Roger" "Roger," "over and out." "Switch to the tower." We were clear to land. I was on Knisley's right. The element eased over on my right. We were all but diving at the end of the runway. Just as we passed the end of the runway at about 100 ft. high, Knisley broke up and to the left. I counted 1,001, 1,002 and followed. I saw

Knisley literally throw his wheels out — in the turn. I did too — spaced myself — lowered the flaps — lined up — I was on the runway — opened my canopy — raised my seat — unlocked the tail wheel — taxied to the hardstand — cut my engine — and began to climb out of the cockpit.

I was wilted. My legs were weak. I stood on the wing a minute while holding to the cockpit. Finally, I took the handhold — found the toe step and swung to the pavement. My parachute felt like it weighed a ton. The jeeps picked us up and took us to debriefing.

The remembrance of the sequence of events in my whole life up to this moment had been vivid and easy. I had been uniquely sensitive to other people and my surroundings. Except for bullies and liars, my experiences had been exciting — some awesome — a few with sadness.

No more!

One mission — and I was consumed. My life became two things — survival and destruction. There was no dread or fear — just fact. From somewhere deep inside me — my guts — inside my heart — in my psyche, I knew it would take all I was and was humanly possible to be for me to survive — and more.

What would be remembered now were events —
not necessarily in order of missions. Events that I
experienced or observed or heard from my
roommates — other pilots — in debriefing — wing
men — crew chiefs — armorers — even from my
uncle's squadron (they controlled our homing
station).

WARREN GLENN TRANTHAM

My uncle, Warren Glenn Trantham, was 10 months older than I. In our very early years we grew up together. One evening I was in the officers' bar — a burned-out German Quonset hut, redone. A sergeant, who tended bar sometimes and kept the place straight, touched me on the arm and said there was someone in the kitchen who wanted to see me. It was Warren. I don't remember whether I hugged him or shook his hand. I hope I hugged him. He was thin as a rail. His fatigues just hung on him. I barely recognized him. He was a Tech Sgt., a radio man. He had been one of the first air corps personnel to land during the invasion to help set up a tarpaper airstrip — A 8 — for the 405th.

Now, he had stomach problems. His food wouldn't stay down. Lord, he was thin. He said that one of the first things he saw after landing was a 6x6 truck load — piled to the top — of stiff dead bodies, and that there was a big black fellow sitting on the cab — feet on the bodies — eating his K-rations. Warren said he upchucked.

Warren was one of a few men that could work in the homing station — the repair shop — or the flight line. He went to all his buddies in the homing station and told them, "My nephew, Ponder, is flying with the 510th. If he ever gets into trouble, drop everybody else and help him — even Col. Jackson (the 405th C.O.)."

I went over to see Warren a few times. I walked. I couldn't get any transportation. His squadron was about a mile away. After dark all the enlisted men would be in tents cooking and eating; they scrounged from the Frenchmen and took what they could swipe from the mess kitchen. They sure ate a lot better than I was eating. Some of the men would shake my hand and talk to me. Others would kinda leer at me. I was an officer in the wrong place. I guess they thought I would report them.

One of Warren's buddies pointed out a master Sgt. He said that the Sgt. had been bullying Warren for a long time and that Warren got enough — told the Sgt. to leave him alone. The Sgt. was twice as big as Warren. Two nights ago they finally got into it. His friend said, "You should have seen bird ass (that's what they called him). He beat the living shit out of that bully." The Sgt. was going to take him to the C.O. and get him busted. About 10 of Warren's buddies crowded around the Sgt. and said, "If you go, we're going with you." Nothing happened.

Warren disappeared from time to time to the hospital with his belly. The next time we got together was at Kitzingen, where his C.O. put his office trailer in one end of the hanger so Warren could convert German radios from 220 to 110 current. He used a lot of tin foil out of cigarette packs to make repairs, and he'd get them playing.

Kitzengen was the last time I saw him for another long spell. Back in St. Dizier, when I'd go to see him, I'd get ready to leave and he'd say to wait a minute and return with keys to a vehicle. I began to realize who ran things. Officers only got the credit.

I didn't do the first meeting with Warren justice. I'll try again. When I first looked at Warren, he wasn't just thin, he was kinda pitiful. I could see in his eyes that he was in trouble. The turn-over rate of pilots was pretty high. It was later when I realized that could have been our only meeting. He must have felt that way at the time. What should have been a joyous occasion didn't turn out that way. It was more like, "Bud, hope to see you again."

THE FIVE OF US!

HUGH MILLER

He was from Wisconsin. He was the best pilot of the five. He and Johns were 43C grads from flying training and both were stuck in the training command for a year — towing targets out over the gulf — off the coast of Texas. Both wanted to get away from that drudgery and get into combat. They ended up with us 44C pilots.

Hugh was the nicest, sweetest man you could meet — always laughing and at some point he would kinda purse his lips like he was going to whistle and say, "Ohoooo." The two of us argued almost constantly about where was the prettiest and best place to live in the whole world — I, Western North Carolina, and he, Wisconsin. Neither of us gave an inch, and we had the best time remembering all the reasons why.

He had flown two missions. After the second he came in the tent. It was late afternoon. There were just the two of us. He came over and sat by me on my cot. He said, "Ponder, I've made a mistake. Back home are my mother, a teenage sister, and my little brother. He's 12 now, and I've been like a father to him. We have had the best time together. He's a real corker. You see, I'm their only support, and because of that I could have stayed in the training command. $10,000 (G.I. insurance) I'm afraid, won't get my sister or him through school."

I couldn't help him. I didn't know how.

The next day he was killed on a strafing pass. One of the pilots said that they sawed off most of his left wing. He righted the plane once — then flipped over and went in on his back.

I knew Johns was hurt bad. They had been really close friends. Johns didn't say anything. I didn't either. Nothing to say.

MILTON EUGENE JOHNS

I could write a book about this character, but I'll keep it short as I can. On his first thirteen missions he'd come home with his plane full of holes — one of the planes so badly shot up he landed in the grass by the runway. All that could be salvaged were some instruments out of the cockpit and the engine — the rest was towed to the junkyard. He finally caught on how to keep from getting hit. After each mission he would kinda swagger into the tent — a half grin on his face and say, "Whew, that was pretty close."

Johns was the cutest thing playing poker that you ever saw. He had learned to play poker at Foster Field with a lot of pilots returning from overseas. It cost him $1,100 — which was a small fortune in those days. He'd cover his losses with a personal check which — he would tell the holder — had to be held — first one month — then two — then three — etc. His checks were all good if cashed in the right month.

In our outfit he made that $1,100 back and probably several times over. He was cunning. He'd set his own stage. Before sitting down at the table he would go to the bar and pour a smidgen of bourbon in a glass — and some water — never over two inches — no ice. From the looks of the glass it looked like he might be about half crocked. Some of the other players — of course — were. He kept that half grin on his face all the time. With his legs crossed most of the time — which put him pretty far back from the table — he would get his down cards off the table — shuffle — fondle them for a while — pull them in close to his chest while looking at the others at the table — and then very slowly move the top card over just enough to see the edge of the next one. There were times that he would drop out and times that he would stay. At the end of the game he would still have about one inch left in his glass — and without counting put his winnings in his pocket.

I never sat in on the table where Johns played — too rich for my blood — stakes were too high — and raises were pot limit. I sat in on the nickel or dime game. Each month on payday I would set aside $20 to play poker. When I lost that, I'd wait until next payday to play again. Sometimes it lasted a week and then three weeks — but never a whole month. Poker is fun, and I enjoyed it.

Johns and I went to Paris on a weekend of R&R — rest and recuperation. We saw lots of sights — went to the Montmartre section — to the Louvre, that was mostly barren of paintings. I do remember seeing the "Mona Lisa." She was cracked all over. We would stop in a street side cafe and order a glass of wine and a serving of French bread — at that time the best stuff I ever tasted. This was a good way to rest before the next venture. We didn't get into the "Follies." They were sold out. It seemed that there had to be more GIs in Paris than were in the front lines.

Johns tells of a mission with Lt. Col. Ralph Jenkins — twice our C.O. Jenks was with the 510th squadron: when they were formed at Walterboro,

S.C. — to England — in on the invasion — a tar paper on the French coast, A-8 — then, to St. Dizier. As C.O., he was due a 30-day R&R to the states and travel time — and he flew very little after I got there until he left in mid-November — and the same was true about his flying after his return. No criticism — just fact. But — there was one big difference in flying in the invasion and after we hit Germany — the homeland. In the invasion the German Panzer divisions had about 50% to 60% anti-aircraft capability. Other units — much less. Now, the Panzers were 99% equipped and other units up to 80%.

Major Sanders, operations officer and leader of Johns's section, told Johns that he was putting him in the element so he could take care of Jenks. After they crossed the front lines, Jenks flew a lot of straight and level which had Johns jockeying his throttle all over the place to keep from getting ahead of Jenks. They weren't very high and all at once Johns recognized that they were flying right over a German airfield, which he reported. Nothing happened. When they cleared the field Johns took a deep breath. (I can just hear him say, "Whew, that was pretty close.") Well, Jenks started making a turn and the first thing Johns knew, they were right on top of that airfield again. All hell broke loose. Johns said he took flak evasion up a couple of thousand ft. and could see that Jenks was getting pounded. As quick as they cleared the field, Johns dropped in by Jenks and Jenks asked him about damage to his plane — and Johns said, "Jampit Red 1 — actually, you don't look so good."

At the end of the war Johns went up to group. I sure did miss him. About the only times I saw him then was when he had a job he didn't want to ask anybody else to do.

One day he came into my room. I was getting extra sack time. The weather was all socked in — all planes were grounded, he handed me a packet full of important papers and said that they had to be in a general's office today in Kassel.

We were at Straubing near the Austrian border. The weather was too low to fly cross-country, so I flew rivers and railroads — up the Danube to Regensburg — turned right up the Naab River — caught a railroad, etc. — had to dodge a bridge now and then. When I got to Kassel, I got clearance, hit close to the end of the runway — slowed down immediately — looked back — I was climbing a hill. Those damned Germans had built the damnedest runway I ever saw. A jeep met me. I went to a general's headquarters — got a receipt for my pouch — jeep back to plane — retraced the railroads and rivers. I was sopping wet when I got home. Enough of Johns for now.

CLIFFORD J. MAYER

Cliff hated Episcopalians. I was an Episcopalian — but we were close, good friends. Cliff was Catholic. His mother had died when he was about ten. His stepmother was an Episcopalian and he was sent off to a parochial school. He hated his stepmother.

One day Mayer got a letter from Louisville, KY., his home. He held it up to the light — looked the envelope over real close and finally opened it. After a while he blew through his lips. I asked if something was wrong. He studied me for a moment and then said that his aunt had paid a pretty penny for the priest to say a bunch of prayers for him. — There was a long silence before either of us said anything else — and then he said that he wished she hadn't done it because she couldn't afford it.

One of the later replacement pilots was Lowell A. Welker from the Baptist belt of southern Ohio. He was a rabid fundamentalist and had been taught that Catholics were ogres of some kind — and here was one that he would make captive. Every chance he got — here he would come — right into our tent. He would start grilling Mayer about his beliefs. Mayer never hesitated or faltered in his answers. He showed much more patience than I could have — and much, much more than Welker. I had to arbitrate one issue. Mayer had been taught that no one could be saved outside the Catholic Church. I could tell he was uncomfortable with his stand, and I gave him the opportunity to say, "Yes, I suppose it's possible for others, but it is a lot easier for us."

Mayer, like Johns, got hit with flak on his first 13 missions. He had to belly land his plane on one mission. On another mission he went in on a tank and had fired his guns before he realized it was one of ours. Our troops returned his fire. When Mayer got home, he almost lost control of himself. He'd pace back and forth — tears in his eyes — and saying over and over that he hoped he didn't hit anybody. Finally, he went to Captain Harings and begged him to get in contact with that outfit. Harings tried to put him off, but finally agreed. Mayer hadn't hit any of our people. He was all right then. Mayer and I wrote one another early on. Never got together. He and his wife had a baby girl. She was blind, complications at birth. Cliff died of cancer sometime in the 70s.

STUART WILDE

From New Jersey. Stu, like Johns and Mayer, took a lot of flak in his first 13 missions. I never figured out why 13 was the magic number — why it took the three of them that long to learn how to keep from getting hit.

Stu was on the board for his second mission. He came running to me and asked if he could borrow my helmet and oxygen mask. His was still in the radio shop. Our ear phones and mike were being converted to the British adapter. We had a plug-in coupling to our earphone and another to the mike. The British had only one for both — really not very important unless you had to leave the plane in a big hurry. When Stu returned from the mission, his eyes seemed to be rolling around and around. He had taken a hit in his bubble canopy — all the Plexiglas was gone — except for a few small pieces where it joined the metal frame. He had a little cut on the bridge of his nose. A small piece of flak had entered one side of my goggles — nicked his nose — and went out the other side — leaving the entire middle of the wrap around goggles unbroken.

Stu was not a home-tent lover like the other three of us, but one night we were all sitting around our pot-bellied stove when Stu yelled that he saw a mouse. The stove was on top of some cinderblocks so the stove pipe would reach out the top of the tent. "Right there. The crack between those two blocks on the floor," he says. We each grabbed something to hit with — shovel, poker, piece of wood — and we each hunkered down with our weapons raised. Sure enough, in a minute a poor little bug-eyed two-inch mouse stuck his head out and studied us. He wasn't far enough out to hit. One of us crumbled a small piece of G.I. chocolate and put it about 6" from the crack. We were ready again. Poised. He stuck his head out again. He looked at the chocolate — then up at us — two or three times. Then, all at once there was a flash — he had a piece of chocolate and back in the crack — leaving us still at ready. Well, we laughed and laughed — and Stu said that anything that brave and that hungry sure didn't need to die. We put our weapons down — put down more candy and watched. Out came his head again — looked us over — and very casually walked over to the candy, sat and ate some — and carried some back into the crack. It's always been a puzzlement to me how that mouse knew when we would hurt him and when we wouldn't.

About 30 years after the war, Stu and his wife drove up to our home in a big elegant motor home. They had sold their home — were touring the country — destination was California. Our meeting was an occasion. He was the only one of the 510th that I had seen in all those years.

I was the fifth.

I kinda sat in the catbird seat. I was the only one of us in my section. The other four went into the other section. I was able to learn the whole squadron pretty quick — who were the daredevils — the good leaders — the good pilots — and who you could depend on. This sort of info was filed into the survival part of my brain. I was intent that a dodo not do me in — and we had a few.

My name was on the board again and again and again — always on Knisley's wing. My job as wing man was to protect Knisley's ass — so to speak — not let an enemy plane or any other danger slip in behind us. This gave Knisley the freedom to concentrate on what was ahead — navigating — finding our target or picking one out — coordinating the 3 or 4 flights — assessing damage — etc. I wondered and wondered why he picked me — was it my record? Or was it because I was from the mountains of Western NC with traits and knowledge similar to his? Or, did he just like my looks? I still don't know. I flew my first 22 missions with him.

Ten missions — no hits. Twenty missions — no hits. I had a system based on my instincts how not to get hit. When I was growing up, I hunted squirrels, rabbits, quail, and ducks on the French Broad River. I understood guns — how to load, aim, and when to fire. I understood deflection shots — how to lead the target. It takes time to lead — aim — and decide when to fire. My system — if I was on the ground trying to hit me up here — what would I have to do up here to make me miss from the ground? When I would feel that I had had enough time to fire from the ground, I would slew-skid the plane to one side or the other. Many, many times the shells would burst right where I would have been. In training we were taught to fly straight and level and make coordinated turns. If you flew that way over here, you got hit; the Germans rarely missed our altitude. I figured if I got hit, it would be an unexpected shot — a shot of some distance away that was reaching for me. Sure enough, all those normal shots in my vicinity didn't hit, but that low level, from a distance shot blasted a hole in my left wing that I could have jumped through with my elbows spread out.

Anyway, I had never bragged about not getting hit. I had only counseled some of my good buddies about my system. Along about 30 missions some smart ass realized that I hadn't been hit and began to kid me, "Boy, you're going to get yours, etc." My reply was, "I know I'm going to get hit. The law of averages says I will, but they'll have to slip up on me." They did.

Back to the Saar Valley sector — Saarbrucken — Saar Laurtern — Trier — it was awful. We were losing planes and pilots — sometimes both — seemed like every mission.

One of the pilots we lost was Chwatek, a Pennsylvania coalminer — big fellow — and real pleasant until he took a drink of liquor — then, he was mean as hell. He'd slip up on you and with his first two fingers bent pinch the fire out of your arm or back. Anyway, he got hit in the head, and before he passed out, he turned on the home heading, (in briefing we got a heading to the nearest front lines) — trimmed his ship — gradually lost altitude until he flew into the ground. Another pilot reported that there was no way he could have survived. About 10 days later we got a letter from him — a nurse had written it. He had hit the ground going, at least, 250 mph near a 2nd armored unit. An ambulance with a doctor picked him up. He had both collarbones, right arm, right ribs and both legs broken. We never heard from him again.

Another was Feucht, a new replacement pilot. On his second or third mission he just disappeared.

The mission was the deepest penetration we had made — near Frankfort — a special target. A pilot reported that on the bomb run Feucht headed east into Germany — no sign of damage — no communication. He had an air about him that was different. Some of us decided that he was probably a German that managed to get into training back in the states and was just waiting for a chance to fly a P-47 to a German airfield. The Germans had a good number of our '47s.

It was the same with Capt. Appel. He became C.O. when Jenkens left — lasted less than two weeks — got hit bad — bailed out — and was taken prisoner. Knisley became C.O.

About this time, coming back off a mission, I was told that my left wing bomb was still on. I pulled out of the flight — made some severe turns — pulled up into a stall and fired my 50 cals. — the plane shook all over. Schaffer, the element leader stayed with me. He said he would knock it loose. He came in close and with the end of his right wing tip bumped the bomb several times. The bomb, of course, had been armed. In the cockpit on the lower left side was a handle for each bomb. The handle was attached to a cable and then to a grab hook so that when you pulled the handle up and twisted it into locked position, the grab hook went under a 1/8" copper wire which ran through the shaft of both the front and rear fuse. This kept the propeller on the fuses from turning. When the bombs were dropped the grab hook jerked the copper wire out of the fuse shafts — the propellers would turn so many revolutions and the fuses would detonate on impact. I pushed the left handle down — not knowing whether the grab hook released the copper wire or not. I hoped that the bomb was disarmed.

The control tower finally said that I could land at the field — but after all other planes were in. How much gas did I have? I had previously switched from the main tank to the auxiliary, which was approaching empty. "Switch back to the main and when it runs out, call us." I stayed away from the field — leaned my mixture all but off — cut my RPM until I was barely hanging in the air. "Control, Jampit Red 2. Main tank's empty. Auxiliary needle touching empty." "Start a slow descent to the end of the field. The last flight is in the landing pattern. OK to land, Red 2." I greased as pretty a three point landing as could be made — almost no jolt. I felt the bomb come off. I looked back — the bomb was skidding down the runway and losing speed — and finally eased off the edge of the runway onto the grass. It didn't explode, because I'm telling you what happened.

Our armament officer came barreling down the runway in a jeep behind me — jumped a-straddle of the bomb and screwed out both fuses. He was a heavy drinker — and I don't blame him.

Had the bomb gone off, the St. Dizier airfield would have been closed until the hole could have been filled in. The control tower could have been destroyed because the bomb came to rest right in front of it.

SUSPECTED SABOTAGE

We had heard that there could have been a fine sand put into our fuel supply by infiltrators or sympathizers. An A-24 twin engine night photo plane failed to get off the end of the runway — barely cleared the bank of a canal (on that end of the runway) crashed and burned. A P-38 weather Recce [abbreviation for reconnaissance] had one engine go out — flipped over on its back and burned. The pilot was still alive — hanging upside down — but no one could get to him because of the heat. A P-47 loaded with fragmentation bombs failed to get off — hit the opposite bank of the canal — nothing was left that was identifiable.

I was taking off in the opposite direction. My engine was sluggish. I kept hunching in my seat to get us going. I reached the end of the runway — I wasn't flying — I used the last foot — pulled us up — jerked the wheel lever — and started settling in. I just cleared a fence that was below the end of the runway. I was blowing heavy black smoke. I was all but on the ground. The fence on the opposite side of the field was coming up. One of the most difficult things I ever did in my life was to push the stick slightly forward — lower my nose — to gain just barely enough more speed to hop over the fence. I settled back down on the other side. Coming up was a brick home with three trees in the yard. I dare not try to turn. I skidded to the right just enough to miss the trees. I began to climb — little by little. I was miles from the end of the field. The squadron had formed up and was headed out. "Jampit Red 1 — Red 2. I'm airborne and circling back toward the field. What do I do now?" Everyone in the whole squadron razzed hell out of me about that — in the air and on the ground. Such things as, "Here I am at 30,000 feet on my back. What do I do now?" The squadron made a big 360 degree turn, and I joined in.

TREE BLASTS

One of Patton's third army armored outfits was pinned down at a river in the Saar sector. He wanted to start an offensive. He called for close support. The Germans were dug in — lots of trenches on their side of the river — armament — tanks — cannons. A little of everything. We were to soften them up, and when we left, the armored outfit was to lay their pontoon bridges down and jump off. We went in low. We could see some of our troops climbing out of fox holes — dugouts — and tanks. Jampit Red 1 was talking to an air force pilot on the ground. By now these air force people had been assigned to most front line units, so that communication with us would be better.

We had some real sharp dudes that planned our missions. Capt. Harings and his crew would receive all the info about a target — where — what was to be destroyed — how heavily defended it was — what weather could be expected — and somewhere along the line — what bomb load to carry — and what kind of bombs. The usual bomb load was 3 five hundred GP (general purpose) bombs. The GPs would not explode on impact if the fuses were not armed. On some missions we carried 3 500 lb. composition "B" bombs — a much higher explosive. When they exploded, they always made a concussion ring — a white circle starting at the bomb and instantly increased in size — probably a 100 feet in diameter — before it dissipated — a beautiful sight to see. Even if they were unarmed, they would still explode if dropped over 4,000 ft.

On other missions we carried two 500 pounders and a belly tank full of gas; on others — we carried two 1,000 lb. bombs — some with up to 5 seconds delayed fuses.

Then, there were the "frag" (fragmentation — anti-personnel) bombs — 3 clusters under each wing. They were very sensitive — no fuses — would explode if dropped just 4 feet — exploded on impact.

Today, we carried a 500 pounder under each wing and a napalm bomb — a big belly tank filled with jellied gasoline. This was the heaviest load we carried — over 2,000 lbs. The next heaviest was a belly tank with gas — still over 2,000 lbs.

The two 1,000 lb. bombs were the same bomb load for medium bombers — B-26, A-26, and B-25. They could carry more 500s. Even now in 1990, it seems impossible that a fighter plane designed for high altitude (30,000 ft. and up) could get off the ground with that much weight — only a 41 ft. wingspan! And, if the engine went out, the plane was so heavy that the glide angle was about 45 degrees to keep airspeed up — with everything jettisoned. Each time we flew — to borrow a phrase — it was like — "mission impossible."

The Germans called the P-47, "Jabo." To me that meant jug — to them it probably meant fire power and destruction [German military slang for Jagdbomber, fighter bomber]. They could not cope with — they feared — the eight 50 cal. guns. In aerial combat, we learned to turn into them when jumped — at any altitude, they fled.

The Germans were dug in across the river. There were a series of trenches around the hill. Trenches zigzag. At each corner was a gun emplacement. We had been briefed to use the napalm — firebomb, on the trenches. Go in two ships at a time and spread the fire as far as possible. Knisley and I lined up on one end of a trench. I spaced myself well behind him. We slowed our speed and went down to the ground — just skimming the top of the trench. Knisley's was away. He hit the top edge of the trench. There was a big ball of fire that splattered everywhere — lots of it down into the trench. I picked out a corner ahead of Knisley's fire —

dropped my napalm down into the trench. It ran about 30 ft. and slammed into the corner. Fire sprayed everywhere. Most of it ran up the zig to the next corner and then some down the zag past that corner. The burning jellied gasoline would cling to and burn whatever it touched. I saw two soldiers in the zag part running to get out of the fire.

We still had two 500 pounders. We regrouped over our side of the lines. Knisley was talking to the A.F. officer about some panzer tanks in some woods above and to the right of the trenches. He said, "We'll fire an orange marker shell near one that fired at us a while ago." We watched. The shell exploded in a beautiful yellow orange color. We began circling above the forest trying our best to pick out the tank. The Germans were experts at camouflage. There was no flak. The Germans were hiding. To shoot at us would give their position away. Knisley and I circled lower and lower — our speed greatly reduced — until we were right in the tops of the trees. All at once the tops of the trees directly under us and all around us just disintegrated. My heart jumped up into my mouth. I knew my ass was done shot off. Knisley yelled, "What in the hell was that?" Knisley had broken left. I had broken right. I didn't see him. I didn't care. I needed a minute to collect myself. "That had jarred my grandmaw," to use a mountain expression, "I had had the shit scared clean out of me."

I began a slow climbing turn to the left — back toward our lines. "Jampit Red 1 — Red 2. What's your location?" "I see you," he said.

I followed Knisley in on our bomb run. Then we strafed gun positions and any place we thought a man could hide. I was glad to see my tracers start firing. That meant we had about 50 rounds left in our guns. We always saved that much ammo in case we were jumped by the jerries on the way home.

We found out what happened. Some of our own artillery which was back some ways from the river had fired those shells. The shells were equipped with proximity fuses and would detonate when they got into the tops of the trees. Some dumb bastard back there saw that smoke shell and must have decided it was meant for him to fire — a bit trigger happy I'd say.

Lord only knows why Knisley and I didn't get hit by our own artillery.

This mission was called a 405th group mission. Don't know why exactly. We left the field 20 minutes apart — but we did work in the same area. I can remember only one other mission that was supposed to be a group mission — we were to escort a box of A-26s to their target. We had our three 500 pounders and before we reached the target we were to pull ahead and soften up the place so the A-26s wouldn't get hit so bad. Hell! When we got through there was nothing left for them to bomb.

I never flew in a group formation as such.

Back to Patton's mission. He was elated. When we left the target area, his armored outfit jumped off. They had no problem pontooning over the river, and, in fact, according to his letter of commendation to us, only met token resistance in the whole area. His headquarters was then in Rheims — not very far away from us. He was so pleased that he sent our group 90 cases of champagne.

Several nights later, when the weather socked in, our squadron had a party. At the appointed time we walked into the old burned out German Quonset hut that had been resurrected for our officers club. The place was clean as a pin, and the tables set up with several bottles of champagne in the center of each. Capt. Stith was playing the piano — all the new hits from back in the states — we got the new ones once a month — and some of the good oldies. At every song fest we would keep clapping and begging for George Orange to sing "Danny Boy." When George walked up to the piano to stand by Stith, everyone would get very quiet — even the drunks. Stith would do the lead-in.

HEADQUARTERS
THIRD UNITED STATES ARMY
OFFICE OF THE COMMANDING GENERAL
APO 403

26 January, 1945

My dear General Weyland:

Please accept for yourself and pass on to the officers and men of your command the sincere appreciation and admiration of myself, and the officers and men of the 3rd Army, for your magnificent cooperation in the reduction of the Ardennes salient.

As usual, we feel that the great successes achieved are the result of the unselfish cooperation and comradeship existing between the Air and Ground troops.

We look forward to bigger and better victories in the immediate future.

Most sincerely,

G S Patton Jr,

G. S. PATTON, JR.,
Lieut. General, U. S. Army,
Commanding.

Commanding General XIX Tactical Air Command
THRU Commanding General 9th Air Force
APO 696
U. S. Army

George had a soft, beautiful tenor voice — he'd close his eyes — move his head slightly from side to side and begin — and as he reached for the higher notes his chin would come up — his head tilt a little to the left side — no more beautiful sound have I ever heard. He sang from inside of himself — a touch of pure perfection. He would always bring tears to my eyes and chilly bumps all over. Doc Milligan would have to wipe his eyes too — and lots of others.

Deep down, I suppose that of all the pilots shot down, I missed George the most — even Knisley — even Miller.

I missed "Danny Boy."

The corks started popping — everyone shooting at something on the ceiling. Before too long I noticed Johns. He had a problem. His eyes were already glazed, but he was getting a big charge out of shooting corks at something on the ceiling. Every time the Sgt. would come by with more bottles, Johns would turn around in his chair and capture another bottle. The problem was that every time he popped a cork he'd catch the overflow in his glass — then he'd have to drink enough out of his glass to hold the next overflow. I found Mayer and said, "Son, we've got to get Johns out of here." We urged him — and again — and again. But he'd just say, "One more shot." Then, after a few more aims and "booms," the next turn for another bottle — we caught him before he hit the floor. He looked up into my face and then into Mayer's and said, "I've got to go to the toilet."

We knew our time was short. Mayer on one side and I on the other held him under the armpits and with some effort engineered him through the door to the outside — which was colder than hell. "I'm going to the toilet," Johns said. The outdoor privies were over on the other side of a deep gully (ditch). "I'm going to the toilet," Johns said again. Mayer and I decided that there was no way we could maneuver the ditch and reach the five (or six) hole privy. (On one door was a picture of Hitler framed in a toilet seat).

Our actions had to be fast. Mayer got behind him and held him up while I unbuckled his belt — unzipped his britches and got his pants and shorts down. Mayer and I each held a hand and an elbow — eased him to a squatting position over the edge of the ditch and told him to go to it. In a minute or so he said he was getting sick. Mayer and I yanked him up and bent him forward enough to miss his downed britches.

Mayer got behind him and held him up until I ran for some toilet paper. We got him cleaned up and put him to bed. He was asleep before we got him tucked in.

During the night my eyes popped open. Someone was moving in our tent. I eased my right hand under my flight jacket pillow and palmed the hilt of my 45 — and listened. I heard a chain jingle on metal — then a glug, glug, glug. I thought of Johns. It had to be him. Was I sure? He went to the next cot/bunk — the chain and the glugs again. Then, I heard him walk up to my cot. I said real sternly, "What in the hell you want?" The most pitiful sound I ever heard said, "Waaater."

I reached my canteen — unscrewed the cap — found his hand — he drank it all.

THE COUNTER ATTACK

It was the week with Christmas in it. The weather was socked in. We were grounded. We mobilized. I was put in charge of a platoon. Every man had a gun of some sort. We drilled. There were squad leaders — all by rank. If the German push came our way — we were ready — with what pistols and carbines could do against tanks. It was very possible that once through our frontline the Germans would fan out and some of them would veer our way. St. Dizier was an old airfield with concrete runways and a prize to be had.

Each day there was always a crowd in the ready room — listening to the news — for the weather to break. We were needed — needed bad. Harings didn't know where the front line was now in that sector. He said the Germans were probably on the way to Antwerp — our major supply depot. If they were, there were no troops or armor to stop them. That had to be their main target. Maybe the 3rd army — the first under Hodges — the British (if they could get Montgomery up off his ass) and/or the Canadians could form a pincher movement and cut the salient in two.

The weather to our west was beginning to break — another day — two at the most — we'd be in the air. As I remember, it was the day after Christmas. Our schedule was set — eight ship flights would leave the ground every 20 minutes. Each squadron took turns getting their eight off on time.

Knisley led our first mission — the other section. I was not with him. After Jenkins returned from R&R, Knisley started flying every mission. He had been an excellent C.O. He was no longer in charge. He had to be upset. He probably felt that if Jenkins wouldn't fly, by damn he'd lead them. When he hit the ground — was debriefed — the other section was on the board — by rank, he would erase someone's name and put himself on.

Some of the older pilots didn't like Knisley. He was hard to know. No one could get close to him. In fact, even though I was his wingman and flew all those missions with him, while on the ground he only spoke directly to me a couple of times. I understood. He had a job. I had a job — and that was it.

I was so proud of him on one mission. At briefing he stood up before us and said, "I've been noticing that some of you are wasting some bombs (I had too). Do you realize that these bombs are made back in the states — have to be transported to a dock — loaded on a ship — spend days on the ocean — be unloaded at another dock over here — and be transported all the way up here to our field. Let's make every one count. Today, we're carrying two 1,000 pounders with delayed fuses (we had a low ceiling). Our target is a railroad roundhouse that is an ammunition dump. So that we don't waste any of these bombs, we'll go in two ships at a time. Ponder and I will go in first. Don't pay any attention how heavy the flak is on your bomb run — make a good hit. That's all. Let's go."

The bombs were fused for delayed firing because the ceiling was low and without a delay we would be caught in our own bomb blast. The area around the roundhouse was densely populated — two and three story buildings. Knisley and I were down to the rooftops — at the railroad dropped down farther — lined up to broadside the roundhouse, clicked our bombs loose so they would penetrate the wall as near to ground level as possible — broke left — 1001, 1002, 1003, 1004 — what a sight to behold — absolutely beautiful. The whole roundhouse went off and up into the clouds. The concussion seemed to push everything out in a circle — then after a beat, beat, beat — all the roofs in that circle went straight down to the bottom. Near the outer edge of the circle there were some walls still standing, and occasionally we would see one more topple over to the ground. Knisley and I circled several times to admire our work, and the colors in that blast were just fantastic.

Knisley drank too much at night — another reason some didn't like him. He upchucked a few times after he went to bed. His tent mates moved out to other tents.

But, in the mornings, outside of being a little bleary-eyed and red-faced, he was raring to go. He was all business. He didn't care whether he was liked or not. While leading his squadron, he was methodical. He was aggressive when the bombing and strafing started. Flak didn't seem to bother him. He said at a briefing one time that he saw on one mission — each mission — more flak here than he saw altogether in the Pacific on all his missions.

I have already said he was a wheelhorse of a pilot. There were no better. Maj. Sanders was in his class. Both were excellent pilots.

On another mission we were loaded with our three 500 pounders and were looking for a target of opportunity. We had our bombs armed and Knisley led Red Flight lower and lower. All at once the leader of Blue Flight, our top cover, started yelling, "Bandits — bandits — bandits." I jettisoned my bombs. I saw Knisley going to full power. I knew water injection was coming. "About 30 of them," Blue Flight leader yelled. They had come from out of the sun so they would be hard to see. They had dived from a high altitude. Knisley and I turned skyward in a steep climb. A ME-109 dived past us at great speed. Knisley winged over and the dog fight was on. No doubt the German pilot expected us to turn away instead of into him. Now, we were on his tail. He pulled into a sharp turn to the left. Knisley followed — pulling wisps of white vapor trails from the tips of his wings. I fell to the inside of Knisley. I was looking back — up — to the sides. My job was to protect Knisley. I couldn't let another German get in behind us. I caught a glimpse of other planes diving. The ME-109 half snapped into a dive to the right — then left into a climb — back to the right — half way in his turn he dived again. I was inside Knisley — then outside during all of this — never very far away. Up went the 109 in a half loop — and down — down — down — he was going to the deck. No. He was going to try to climb out. I suppose he had been taught that the 47 couldn't climb with lighter aircraft. Up-up he went. I was sitting right beside Knisley — the 109 in my gun sight — waiting for Knisley to stall out. He still had his two wing bombs on — the belly bomb was the only one that came off when we were jumped. I had made my mind up that when Knisley stalled, I would continue pursuit. I wasn't supposed to, but I was. The 109 had reached the top of his climb and began turning left. I saw Knisley's 50s belching. He raked the 109 from the top — behind the engine — and down through the fuselage near the cockpit. The German pilot ejected from his plane. Out he came — seat and all. (The Germans had perfected the ejection seat. The pilot hit a button and a charge blew seat and him straight up.) The seat then separated from the pilot as he began to go down. He pulled his rip cord — the chute came out but never did open. It only wavered back and forth as he fell.

We didn't have ejection seats, but we had backpack parachutes. Knisley had apparently put one or more hits into the German's seat pack chute.

Knisley was jubilant. He was laughing and I could see him yell. He held up a clenched fish and shook it at me and said, "Let's go home."

Lord, that had been fun! Relaxing! The constant flak tended to get us down. We didn't know which burst would have our number on it. Almost all missions were flak — flak — flak.

This moment I was elated — tingling. I had just seen the monster turn, dive, and climb with one of the best airplanes in the world — and with two wing bombs still on — another 1,000 lbs.

Bombs! — I guess I'd better tell him. I wasn't supposed to tell Knisley anything. He was the daddy rabbit — but, I said, "Jampit Red 1 — did you know you still have your wing bombs on?" The air turned blue. "What in the hell do you mean? Why didn't you tell me earlier? What kind of a damn wingman are you? And blah, blah." Then, he was smiling — his oxygen mask and mine had been off some time so we could wipe the sweat off of our faces. "Never mind," he said, "We'll find a place to dump them. How about that lake up there?" We made a diving swoop — he clicked his bombs loose — and we were headed home.

There was only one sad part about that mission — and I've thought about it through the years — — — — — Knisley didn't stall out.

Now — it was the day after Christmas. On one of his eight ship missions, Knisley was shot down and killed.

When his flight returned — what was left of them — hadn't been gone long — they said that he had led them down through a cloud layer right on top of a nest of Germans. They clobbered him. His plane was on fire — nosed into a dive — he jettisoned his canopy — was trying to stand up in the cockpit to jerk open his backpack chute when he hit the ground — frag bombs and all.

Knisley was gone.

I hadn't been there to look after him.

At the end of the second day we had 8 ships on the ground out of 25 — 2 of them would fly. The ground crews worked all night and on the third morning we had 4 ships that could fly. We had to borrow 2 ships each from the 509th and 511th to fly an 8 ship mission.

On the way in on my first 8 ship mission I was astonished — in one sector — mostly wooded — there were crashed planes everywhere. So many that it looked like a junk yard — graveyard. Most of them were C-47s, the twin engine Dakota that was the workhorse in the whole air force. It made me wonder if any C-47s got supplies to Bastogne. The Germans had had a hey-day.

We flew under the overcast not far off the ground. Some of the hills were still sticking up in the clouds. We found a long convoy of all kinds of vehicles snaking along a curvy road. One spot that looked like a parking lot is where we dropped our frag bombs. Then we strafed and strafed and strafed. This time straight down the road with the vehicles. We usually made our pass from the side. It was real dark under the overcast and the smoke from all the fires we set made it all but impossible to see at times.

If we just could have flown earlier, if we could have met their breakthrough, we could have saved lots of lives.

They knew when to jump off. The Germans are a bunch of smart bastards — damn their souls.

It seems like we lost 9 pilots during this time — either killed or M.I.A.

Through all this — I still hadn't been hit — the only pilot that hadn't been. I believe in luck, and I don't believe in luck. What is luck? Being in the right or wrong place at the wrong time, or being in the right or wrong place at the right time. If it was luck and could be measured by a yardstick, I was down to less than a foot. My training and instincts had to mean something. What I did know was that the odds of my not being hit were getting smaller and smaller.

DOC MILLIGAN

What a superb, wonderful human being. I wish the world were full of people like him.

He cared. He cared about each one of us. He wept, and still does, for those killed or missing in action.

He did most of his doctoring in the officers' club after the bar opened, except each man in the whole outfit had to go to the infirmary at least once a month for a short arm inspection and let him look at their butt hole.

He studied each one of us pilots. I learned early on what he was doing. He doctored us with liquor. He always managed to have just a little whiskey in the bottom of his glass. He'd look us over — pick out his patient — walk up — put his arm around the pilot's shoulders and say, "Man, how you doing?" After a little chit-chat he'd make a big gesture about emptying his glass and then say, "Come on to the bar with me, I need another drink," like he wasn't through talking to you.

He had a friend behind the bar — Swanson, a blond-headed Swede, that just loved to tend bar.

He was there every night doing his thing. "Refill," Doc would say. "What are you going to have?" if I happened to be his patient. "Barkeep, fix him one of your best," he'd say. Swanson worked off a little table behind and kinda underneath the bar. We'd get a sluggeroo and Doc with just a smidgen.

We had a few non-drinkers. Doc would take them to the bar and ask Swanson what kind of fruit juice he had. "Fix this man a glass of your special fruit juice," he'd say. It would be some kind of canned juice, but heavily spiked with the 150 proof alcohol out of the infirmary. He'd stand around and talk until you had a couple of drinks and then he was off to find another patient.

Better to knock the edge off our nervous system with alcohol rather than pills. If he had started pushing pills, we would have all thought that something was wrong with us.

Not too long a time — the Bulge I guess — Swanson was shot down.

Through my life I have noticed that some men just stand out above others. They are compassionate and truly love their fellowman. They start from a different place than the rest of us. Doc Milligan came at me with his heart and soul. I felt like he was a keeper of part of my heart and soul.

Doc is 80 now. I saw him 14 months ago in Albuquerque. He's still busy — still working and caring for people. After the war Doc returned to his practice in Seattle. In a relatively short time his wife died. He was lost. He quit his practice. He couldn't stand Seattle any longer. Some of his doctor friends down in California begged him to come down, and they'd help him set up another practice. His patients were people with money. Treating them was boring — too many airs and demands. So, he moved over to Salinas where everyone was poor. When the Vietnam War came on, he did two tours over there — treating civilians — not the military.

When he became 70 and had some thoughts about retirement, he said, "It's time that I did something for the people in the little town of Fremont, Nebraska, where I grew up. I owe them a whole lot." He returned to Fremont after all those years — bought two buildings on the main street and opened a clinic. The previous medical treatment had been in Omaha — forty miles away. After two or three years he got a young doctor to come in and help him — another few years a second young doctor. Guess what? At the age of 78 he started another clinic in another small town. I think those corn huskers should change the name of their state to Milligan. Oh! How he loved the Irish ditties. He loves his forbears — he loves those Nebraskans — he loves God's people, each and every one — and he loved and loves each one of us in the 510th. Whataman! — strong-minded — gallant — sweet — kind — generous — loving — happy, one can see it in his eyes. He knows, God bless him, that he's made a difference in this world.

The 510th had its first reunion after 37 years, and each year since, Doc brings his black bag full of pills to help with our aging complaints. I hug him and kiss him on the cheek each time I see him, for what he did for me — and for all those others that have crossed his path.

A few more odds and ends about St. Dizier.

During the Bulge our supply lines were cut off. Our cooks had to rely on emergency provisions — C rations — dehydrated everything. Ordinarily, the food was transported to the officers club — same food — served in plates. Made it taste better. Now, there was no way to transport C-rations after being cooked. Everyone ate in the mess tent. We officers took our mess kits and canteen cup with us. We would get in line — dip our utensils in a tub of boiling water — and when we were served — everything ran together — potatoes — carrots — spinach — beets — powdered eggs, and they would have green streaks in them. When we got hungry enough, it didn't taste near as bad as we first thought it did.

To get a box of K-rations — about the size of a Cracker Jack box — was a treat. It was fun opening them up, because you never knew what you would find — a small can of meat or eggs cooked with ham tid-bits — cheese and crackers — sometimes sweet fruit — maybe a bite of candy — and sometimes a few cigarettes.

That's when I learned that Capt. Pete Harings was drinking powdered milk. He had stomach problems — ulcers probably — and Doc had put him to drinking milk. He'd put a couple of spoons in a glass — fill it with water — and stir and stir. It would foam up. He'd take a sip — and after a bite of food turn the glass up and drink about half of it.

Lt. Murray was a pilot that lived in a tent diagonally across from ours by himself. He was a sallow, wrinkled faced fellow with tousled hair — never did comb it. No one would live with him. Every evening he would be standing by the officer's club door waiting for it to open so he could get to the bar for a drink — and he'd drink all evening. Most nights he peed in his bed — get up the next morning — build a fire in the pot-bellied stove — and drape his blankets on cots around the stove to dry out during the day. I never knew why Doc didn't send him home.

I drew runway alert a couple of times. Each squadron rotated this duty. Four planes — four pilots — and four crew chiefs. We were to protect our field from a surprise air attack. There was a tent with a pot-bellied stove that would hold only four people. On arrival the pilots would climb into the planes — make a thorough check — start the engines and warm them up. The crew chiefs stayed in the tent. After the engines were hot we cut them off and just sat there until we were cramped. Then we'd climb down and go to the tent. The crew chiefs would go get in the planes. Our flight leader was Pawlek, a most handsome dude — looked just like Ray Milland, the movie actor.

The tent had a wooden floor and a radio to the control tower. We stayed fully clothed all the time — parachutes buckled on and all. As soon as we entered the tent, Pawlek would take his seat on one of the two wooden benches and start dive-bombing. He'd get his pocket knife out — the big blade had a keen point — put a wooden match on the floor — lean over — sight down the knife — release the knife and say "oooooa, boom" — over and over and over — sometimes he would giggle.

I learned to take six coins about the size of quarters — hold them upright between my thumb and first three fingers — and with my thumb roll the outside coin over the other five to the inside without upsetting the other five.

After a good long spell, Pawlek would look up — close his knife — and say, "Let's go warm those babies up again."

This procedure went on for hours. When we were finally relieved, it sure felt good to get out of those backpack chutes and stretch our tired muscles.

It had snowed for several days. When planes were not taking off or landing, hundreds of French civilians, men and women, would shovel the snow to one or the other side of the runway. They couldn't get it all off. During the day there would be some melting and at night it would freeze into a coat of glazed ice.

At the bare hint of daybreak I was headed down the runway with a load of frag bombs. Just as I blew my tail up — some pilots kept their tail wheels down — I felt with the tail up I could gain speed faster — there was a misfire in the engine — the whole plane shuddered. The point of no return was getting close. I thought, "If it does it again in the next couple of seconds, I'm pulling everything

— otherwise I'm committed." It did! I pulled everything — throttle and turbo — brakes were of little use on the ice. I yelled into the mike for the next two ships to hold it up while I dropped my flaps — opened my cowl flaps — everything that might slow me down. I began essing down the runway. I had my essing figured perfectly to go into the marshaling area on the other end of the runway. I had it made. Then, I saw him — a damn stupid, son of a bitch M.P. standing in the middle of the entrance to the marshaling area — guarding the damn runway. His motorbike was to the side — but not that bastard. Not only was that dumb son of a bitch in the middle of the place I had to go — he froze. He couldn't run. I knew with that big wind milling propeller, he didn't have a chance. I should have gone on — with those frag bombs — but, I couldn't. I was close to stopping — but not on ice. I pedaled the right brake enough to miss him and went off the end of the runway. I barely went over the bank — but enough so that the left landing gear folded up — the frag bombs were on the ground — maybe it was the snow that kept them from exploding — I don't know — nothing I had anything to do with. I sat real still — saw the MP running toward me to help. He saw the frag bombs and ran faster the other way. I slid my canopy back — very gently, unbuckled my seat belt and shoulder straps — very slowly and calmly put a foot in the seat — held to the windshield — eased my right foot onto the right wing — then the left — lowered my butt to the wing — eased to the back edge of the wing and dropped off to the ground. To this day I have never forgiven that M.P. He's still a dumb son of a bitch — wherever he is.

A jeep picked me up. When I walked into the ready room, Capt. Haring looked at me — came toward me — began to cry — and hugged me. No word was said.

I was put on the next 8 ship mission.

One day while we were grounded, I walked over to see Warren. He gave me a tour. First, we went to the back shop — radio repair shop — where he sometimes worked. He introduced me to several of his buddies who were standing at benches working mostly on radio equipment out of the planes. When a Tech. Sgt. on the flight line had a problem he couldn't fix, the equipment was brought to the back shop and swapped out for some that had been repaired.

Next, we went to the "Homing section." It was a van type trailer with a tongue on it so it could be pulled by a 6x6 truck. We climbed inside and Warren introduced me to the three men inside. He said, "Fellows, this is my nephew that I've been telling you to take care of." "We've been listening for you," one of them said. Near the middle of the van one of them sat at a table with all kinds of instructions and writing materials on it. About 6" or 8" over the table was a wheel about 2' 0" in diameter which was fastened to a shaft that ran through the top of the van. An antenna was on top of the shaft; beyond the wheel was a radar screen — the first one I had ever seen. The Sgt. told me to watch the screen and as he turned the wheel blips would appear. "That's so and so; I gave them a heading a while ago. I'll start bringing them down under this mess in about another minute. When I get them under the overcast and about two miles from the field, I tell them to switch over to the tower."

Radar in its infancy.

On a typical mission we had the homing station and a regional control whose call letters were "Rosalee." Rosalee was made up of three stations at least 50 miles apart. If we needed help, we could get a fix. It went something like this, "Rosalee, Rosalee, Jampit Red 1, would you please give me a fix?" "Roger, Jampit Red 1, this is Rosalee. Give me a transmission over." Jampit Red 1 would then count (slowly) to ten and back to one without breaking the voice vibrations. "Jampit Red 1, this is Rosalee. Here are your coordinates. Over." "Jampit Red 1, Roger. Over and out."

During the voice transmission each of the three stations would take a fix, and where the three fixes intersected was where we were.

Other times when returning on a mission, Jampit would call for a heading. We would fly that heading until we got in range, and then we'd switch to the homing station. Rosalee and the homing station were always there. They never failed us.

On another day, after lunch — we were still socked in — Johns, Mayer, and I decided to get some exercise and walk east over to a river. We started walking down the river bank, and right near the edge of the river bank we found a German bomb. The bomb was at least two feet in diameter and probably 5 to 6 feet long. It had a thin, flimsy outer casing that was broken open in the middle — around the casing. Inside, it was plumb full of anti-personnel bombs about 12" long. They were somewhat tear drop shaped with a fin on the trailing edge and a propeller on the nose that primed the fuse. I picked one up — looked it over real good — decided to throw it out into the river — arced it up enough so the propeller would turn enough revolutions — damndest explosion you ever heard. Then, we took turns. On top of the water we began to see a real silvery fish — some up to 12" long. I said that we ought to try to get a mess of them to take home with us. We found a couple of sticks long enough to reach out a little ways into the water. Then, one of us would take a bomb upstream and throw it near our bank. In a few minutes the fish would come floating down, and we were able to rake some of them to the bank. I cut a small limb from a tree with my pocketknife — trimmed it up — left part of a branch at the bottom — slipped the little end through the gills and out the mouth of the fish. After throwing about 50 bombs, we took our mess of fish and went home. We got the Sgt. to fry them for us. The stench was awful and the taste was worse. We couldn't eat the damned things.

ZWARTBERG, BELGIUM Y-32

The breakthrough had been stopped. The Germans had lost lots of trucks and supplies — some tanks — some prisoners, but they still had a good number of their Panzer divisions. We faced 6 at any given time — and according to Cpt. Harings — 2 or 3 more in reserve. The front lines were now at Aachen and Duren — the edge of the homeland. At night the Panzers maneuvered around until we never knew for sure what we were facing. The Germans — all of them — military and civilians were now fighting more fiercely than before. We were beginning to enter their soil. Our orders changed. We heard of the massacre of our prisoners at Malmedy. Through the underground we heard that a pilot that had bailed out after getting hit was attacked by German women before he could unbuckle his chute. They rocked him and they beat him with sticks. They kicked him all over until he was dead.

Our orders now were not to try to escape at every opportunity, but if we could, to give ourselves up to any German air force personnel — second, to the Volkstram [Volkssturm, the Nazi militia of old men and young boys called up in the final months of the war], the peoples' army — never to the SS Troopers — and stay put — only to give our parole for a specified time — to help a fellow prisoner.

Up until now the 9th army had been a paper army — general staff that issued orders — counter intelligence stuff. The Germans believed they faced another whole army, but there was not a unit (fighting) in it.

The ninth army was activated. From the Bulge we learned a lesson. Montgomery was supposed to protect the north flank of General Hodges 1st army. Montgomery did little to help Hodges during the breakthrough. The 2nd armored division and other units were moved from Patton's third army. Units were moved from Hodges 1st army. Six P-47 groups and one P-51 group were moved to the new 9th army. The array facing the Germans now looked like this — on the left, the Canadian Army — then, the British — the ninth — Hodges 1st — Patton's third — and in the extreme right, the seventh army. These armies faced the Germans from the North Sea to the Alps.

Immediately after the Bulge a convoy of trucks showed up. We were told to get our personal belongings and load up. We left everything else behind — tents — officers club with tables and chairs. Only the bare essentials were loaded on the trucks.

We now had about 12 planes that would fly; the twelve pilots gave us a day's start and then flew a mission on the way to Zwartberg.

I nearly forgot one very essential item — our cots. Each pilot folded his cot — tied it together — put identifying marks on it — and watched it like a hawk. I strapped mine to my B-4 bag. The reason was that the more you slept in it, the more the canvas molded its shape to your body, particularly for your shoulders and hips. It took a long time to break in a new cot enough to sleep comfortably.

We left St. Dizier right at daybreak. Before too long we got on the "Red Ball" highway — a major supply route to the front. We followed the red balls that were stenciled on buildings, or wherever, for several miles away from the front — then off to the right and into Belgium. Most all the roads were very rough and filled with holes. Our butts pounded the wooden seats — the seats were actually like benches — and we sat side by side and were packed together. Our truck had a canvas top, and we could only see out the back or a little through the rear window of the cab. Up in the day with all the motion, some of us began to sleep. It was really funny to watch another pilot sitting straight up — be sound asleep — and watch his head bob up and down. When we would hit a hole, his head would fly back and then pop forward to his chest. I don't know why it didn't break our necks. Mayer and I started swapping up — I'd put my head in his lap and he would rest his arms and head on my shoulders. In a little while we would swap again.

After dark we stopped in a village. Some of us went upstairs in a building that had been some Belgian family's home. In one room there were enough bed frames — no mattress or springs — only slats or boards in the bottom. The British had stayed there before us. They had shit in a corner and on one bed frame, I couldn't think of but two reasons they would do that — they were upset at being moved out — or they were just that damn dirty.

The next morning we began to see stockpiles of ammunition — shells — boxes — all kinds of stuff — stacked like cordwood piles — all very neat and easy to get to. We knew we were in Montgomery's section. These piles went on for miles. We were told that Monty would advance a few feet and then regroup — moving all those piles ahead one pile. In all fairness to the British, they had been fighting this war for 4 years. They had lost thousands of men.

The ones left had seen action in lots of campaigns — Dunkirk — North Africa — wherever. Monty didn't want to lose one more soldier if he could help it.

Zwartberg was mainly a coal mining town. There was no airfield there. Our army engineers had come in — graded a strip of land out in the boondocks — bolted metal sections together for the runway — and were still working on the taxi strips and hard stands. The mud was knee deep in places. It was like a miracle. A few days ago this was farmland — now it was an airfield. When the planes arrived, all three squadrons had to park the planes in the marshaling area at each end of the runway. In a couple of days the engineers had finished the rest.

Our airstrip was top secret. We were told not to tell anyone where it was. We were close to the front lines. At night the artillery battles would light up the horizon in a semi-circle around us. That didn't bother us, but the buzz bombs did. A buzz bomb was a bomb with wings on it and a solid fuel engine to move it along. [Officially named V1, first used by the Germans in June 1944, they were pilotless jet planes packed with explosives which were to crash upon impact. They were inaccurate and mainly targeted at cities, particularly London.]

They flew about 500 ft. high. They crossed over our field coming from two different launching pads — one toward Antwerp — another toward Liege. Their sound was unnerving until you got used to them. Day and night — coming toward the field, they went putt---putt---putt---putt; over the field, they went putt-putt-putt like the engine was about to quit; going away they went putt------putt------putt------putt, all caused by the speed of sound added or subtracted from the speed of the bomb — which wasn't very fast. To the southwest of us, was a large area that was restricted to flying except for the British air force. Their fighter pilots intercepted the buzz bombs — flew alongside — eased their wingtip under the little wing of the bomb and flipped the bomb over. The bombs were controlled by gyro instruments and when placed at an angle of 60 degrees would tilt. The bomb would then nose down and explode on impact.

All of the officials in the coal mine lived in a newly built complex shaped like a rectangle with one end left off. A street went up one side — turned by the president's home and down the other side — with grass and trees between the two streets. The officials were assigned housing by their titles in the corporation — the president and two vice-presidents had their own house — all the rest were duplexes. Mayer, Johns and I stayed about 1/3 of

the way up on the right side with Desire' and
Nanette Schoofs and daughter — 4 or 5 years old
— named Ady. Our duplex was two stories — 3
bedrooms and bath upstairs — LR — Dining Room
and Kitchen, down. Oh! What luxury! A bathroom
with ceramic tile on the walls and a bathtub — and
plenty of hot water. The three of us took turns
soaking in the tub full of the hottest water we
could stand. When we started to wrinkle, we'd get
out.

At St. Dizier we had had a shower that was a belly
tank mounted on a framework with a coil inside
that ran down into a coil inside a pot-bellied stove.
No cold water — just hot. Sometimes the water
would be almost boiling. We would barely crack
the valve under the tank to get a dribble of water
— handful by handful wet our bodies — soap up
— and handful by handful get the soap off. The
water in the tank was pumped in from a truck.

The Schoofs were wonderfully nice people — but
scared to death. Germans had lived with them
before us. Desire' had English as a foreign
language in college, and I had had French; between
his English and my French, we barely made out.

On the third evening there was one rap — military
rap — on our door. I opened it and there stood
Desire' with Nanette behind, holding Ady's hand

and Ady was peeking around her father. He said, "Today, mine woman she - - - -." I said, "What?" I frowned. He tried again. Finally, he pointed at something in the room. I stepped back. He came in and went to the mantle and moved some objects that were on it. I got it. She had insisted that Desire' tell us what she had touched. I was furious, "This is your home. We are only guests. She can touch anything in here." He flew out the door. He knew I was upset. Then, I reverted to a common language — hand signs. I pointed at her — pointed to the mantle — went over — got an object — offered it to her. Desire' smiled. Between my hands — English and French — I made him understand that she could come in our room — move anything she wanted to — and clean all she pleased. This was her home.

We had another problem, if one could call it that. After the first night, the three of us would go to the side door (back door) enter the hall and take our muddy shoes off. The next morning — regardless of when we came in — all pairs of shoes would be cleaned and shined. Desire' met us one night and said, "Mine woman, she needs - - - - ." We finally settled on shoe polish. I said that I wouldn't bring any polish, because she wasn't supposed to clean our shoes. He insisted. We brought all we could find.

All three of us brought Ady little gifts — candy — gum — and the like — Desire' tobacco — Nanette, anything with food in it.

One evening Desire' knocked on the door and invited us downstairs to the living room. We were now truly guests. Nanette had something to drink — can't remember. We tried to chat — all were doing much better. Ady either sat in her mother's lap or would stand with her head over in her mother's lap. She was bald-headed — had had scarlet fever and lost all of her hair. Could have been one of the reasons for her shyness. Even so, she was a beautiful child.

Another evening in the living room, I offered Ady something, and she walked over and took it out of my hand. I had arrived.

After the war was over, I visited the Schoofs again — another story. Nanette opened the door. She was beside herself. She was smiling and laughing and in good English said, "Please come in." While we were living there, she rarely said a word of any kind — much less English. Now, she could speak English better than Desire'. While we were there, she got Desire's text books and taught herself. I was home again. It dawned on me that a person can have several homes. When you get there, you know it. It's a place of mutual something or other

— wanted, needed and respected, loved. To be home is an extraordinary happening in one's life.

We had a glass of wine before dinner, and with dinner. The table was set with beautiful china, silver, and glassware, and a tablecloth. I asked how all this survived the war. Nanette said that they buried most of it.

Nanette served a beef roast, potatoes, peas — Desire' carved — she served the vegetables. Hmmmm, delicious. And Ady was laughing too. Her hair had begun to grow back.

I walked into Cpt. Harings's briefing room. My heart sank. That's a good description — it's when you see something, and all of your insides begin to gather in the pit of your stomach. Straight across the plains and over the Rhine River lay the Ruhr Valley [Germany's main industrial area in the western part of the country] — solid red on the flak map from Weser and Dusseldorf for miles up the Ruhr. I looked away and looked back at the map two or three times. I had flown in flak where there were blobs of red on the map — and it had been thicker than hell. But! Solid red? No way baby. No one could fly in that for long. It was kinda like looking in a mirror — or into the future. My days were probably numbered.

I was good at my job — I was a professional destroyer — buildings, planes, tanks, trains, trucks, cars, and people, anything that I could get my gun sight on. I said to myself, "Ok, Bud, it's going to take all you've got left to make it past the Ruhr." Then, I made a vow to myself: If I made it through that solid red, I was going home — and stay home — even if I had to dig ditches to do it.

Then I had another thought: I'd kinda like to be back in the Saar Valley sector — hotter than hell — but I knew what to expect. Here — there was an unknown.

The plan was set. Since no one could get Monty and his British Army to move, it was left up to the Canadian Army on his left and the Ninth Army on his right to jump off. Each was to fan out to protect their flanks, but the main thrust was toward the Rhine. Near the Rhine they were to turn toward one another in a pincher movement that would surround a large territory full of Germans — and prevent their escape.

The Panzer Divisions were playing checkers with their positions. At each briefing Harings would show us where this or that one was — another might be here or there, but he didn't know for sure.

The 2nd Armored Division — moved from the Third Army — was ready to jump off. They were delayed. Ready again. Delayed again. There were some lakes near Aachen and Duren, and the Germans were letting enough water out of the dams to keep all of the streams at bankfull — and enough in reserve to flood all of the lowlands in case of an attack. It was two or three weeks before the 2nd could push off.

Harings was giving us all kinds of targets. One was a town down in the plains — full of German armor and troops. It was a bright sunny day, and we could see the town in the distance before we got to it — out there — all by itself. For a plane designed as a high altitude fighter, we had learned, by now, how to make it the most accurate dive bomber. We had learned back in the states that at 14,000 feet and 250 mph, if you rolled over on your back and split-essed straight down, the 47 would hit the ground before coming out of the dive. Now we were starting at 4,000 ft. We would pick out our target — fly directly over it — pull the throttle back — and nose up to kill the speed — roll over on our back — and drop the nose through — straight down. We could literally almost drop a bomb down the hole in a smokestack.

We had 16 ships on this mission, and we methodically, each pilot, picked his own target — building by building. It was like pattern bombing — beautiful work. As the last flight finished, the squadron leader said, "Now, that's what I call liberating a town."

Just as we were ready to start strafing, a gaggle of ME-109s and long-nose FW 190s dived through us from out of the sun. We turned into them. Everyone was scattered in all directions. Somebody yelled that he got one. Some of us went back to the town — strafed anything that was left with our APIs (armor piercing incendiary) ammunition. When we finally left, the whole town was burning.

Another mission was on the day when the offensive began. We were to cut four rail lines coming out of Cologne and across the plains to keep the Germans from moving their big rail guns toward the front. Those guns were awesome. They fired shells nearly as big as bombs. The barrels were so long that it took two rail cars to accommodate their length when being moved.

I was Donovan's wingman. We drew Simpkins as our flight leader. We knew we were going to take a ride. Simpkins was one of the older pilots whose luck seemed to be wearing out. It seemed that every time he got below 7,000 ft., he got hit. During briefing when we got our target, Donovan stepped over to me and said, "Ponder, you and I will have to cut those tracks." He didn't say it quietly, either. I glanced at Simpkins. It didn't bother him. He already knew what he was going to do.

At 10,000 ft. the rail lines looked like spokes of a wagon wheel. We were to go in two ships at a time. Simpkins picked our line. He and his wingman made a diving turn to the left, and at about 6,000 ft. lobbed their bombs toward the tracks. Didn't even come close.

Donovan flew until he was lined up straight down the tracks — rolled over and split essed. I spaced myself and followed. I picked Donovan up. He was smaller than a dime. He went down and down and down. There were some scud clouds at about 500 ft. I thought, "The bastard is going to fly into the ground." All this time I was adjusting my rudder trim tab to keep my needle and ball centered. I was about to give up on Donovan when I saw him break his dive. He went under a scud cloud. His bombs hit to the side of the tracks — didn't cut them — but lots of damage. Gun sight — needle and ball. They were right. I clicked my bombs loose — broke my dive — started cranking elevator trim tab — without the help of the trim tab, I was not strong enough to pull the stick back far enough. A glance back — the rails turned back in a coil in four different directions. My air speed was at least 550 mph and probably over 600 mph. I was at the bottom — only 100 to 200 ft. high. I began to climb. I greyed out. Grey out means you can't see because the blood has been forced out of your head from the G (the number of times of the pull of gravity) pull. I've heard other pilots say they blacked out. If you're blacked out, you're unconscious. I couldn't see. I climbed. I could tell by the way my butt was pressed to the seat cushion. I started rolling the elevator trim tab back. I knew that if I didn't get enough I would be going straight up or even over the top onto my back. I couldn't see my airspeed. I didn't want to stall. I let the trim tab out enough until my butt began to get light on the cushion. My vision came back. I was at 7,500 ft. in a climbing turn to the left. I looked ahead and a little left and there was Donovan. He was a daredevil — an excellent pilot. Both of us had greyed out — trim tabbed our way out of the dive. We had truly flown by the seat of our pants.

CHESTER A. BLACK

I nearly forgot to tell what happened to Chester back at the town we liberated. When the German fighters came down through us, Chester latched on to the tail of a ME-109. He was determined. After several climbs, dives, and turns, the German pilot hit the deck and headed straight for Germany. Chester was so close to him that it looked like he was going to chew off the 109's tail. (All of us got to see the film from his gun camera. Each time he fired the camera started and continued to run about 5 seconds after his last shot). Chester fired so many times that the film was almost continuous. They crossed the Rhine and on deep into Germany. Chester said he began to worry about having enough gas to get back. About that time his guns began to fire some tracers — so Chester broke off and headed home. He was terribly disappointed. At the end of the film several of us said almost in unison — you were too close to him to hit him. The vertical distance from the gun sight to the level of the guns was about 4 feet. Chester was firing under the wings of the 109, and the guns were so wide apart on the 47 that he couldn't hit the fuselage.

Chester was from Shaker Heights, Cleveland, Ohio.

When we first started flying off the metal strip, about $1/3$ of the way from the west end the runway was covered with water. On the left side the water was pretty deep. Regardless of the direction of the wind we had to take off west to east and land east to west. Until the engineers got the strip leveled out, there were several hairy situations.

One of them happened as I returned to the field and landed. I made a good three-pointer and began to slow down so I wouldn't be going too fast when I hit the water. The tower said to keep it moving — keep it moving. I knew he meant me. I gunned my engine. Murray had just hit the runway and apparently thought the tower meant him — so he came on down the runway faster than hell. By this time I was moving at a good speed, but Murray overtook me. His big four-bladed propeller cut my tail off for about 3 ft. into 2" metal strips. I was finally able to pull away from that pickle-headed bastard. But, if the man in the tower had kept his mouth shut, it wouldn't have happened anyway.

There were three giant slag piles from the coal mines in our traffic pattern. They stuck way up in the air. While we were on a mission, the fog rolled in and visibility was very poor. Our flight came in under a very low ceiling. We made our normal landing pattern. After we broke, I was feeling my way when one of those slag piles loomed in front of me. I was able to skid to the side enough to miss it.

Returning from another mission, the same type situation happened, only this time the visibility was all but zero. Flares were being fired up into the air at the end of the runway. We finally saw the flares — went down close to the runway — made a slow turn to the left — and listened for someone to hit the runway. We were all on instruments. I saw the flares again. I was too high and coming in at a 45 degree angle to the runway. I turned down the runway — set my gyro compass on 0 degrees — flew one minute — made a 90 degree turn left — flew 30 seconds — made a 90 degree turn left — flew one minute — counted 1001, 1002, to 1010 — made a 90 degree turn left — flew 30 seconds — made a 90 degree turn left. I began lowering the plane — saw the flares again. I was straight down the line and greased her in.

One day after supper, four of us went to Liege — about 40 miles away. We used one of the German cars that just happened to end up in our motor pool. No use to let it set up and rust because the Germans didn't have any gasoline. Liege was blacked out. We parked on the square. There was a lot of noise down on one end. It was a cafe full of 2nd Armored people. They had liberated Liege and had been asked to return by the town officials. They were there for seven days of R&R before heading into Germany. When we walked in, everyone hushed — dead quiet. All eyes were on us. They were a rough looking bunch of cob-nobbers. We went up to the bar. Out of the corner of my eye, I saw a big brute of a looking fellow coming toward us. Even though we were officers, I could just feel that our asses were going to get whipped. This was their place. "Where you boys from?" He asked. "From a P-47 group up the road," I answered. It always seemed I had to be the spokesman because I was the tallest. I was still facing and leaning on the bar. Real mean like he said, "What did you say?" I could feel a tingling between my shoulder blades where I was going to get hit. I turned my head toward him and said good and loud, "A P-47 group from up the road." He let out a war whoop. "Boys, come here," he yelled, "Here they are."

I never met a nicer bunch of fellows. They all gathered around us — shook our hands — patted us on the shoulder — some on the back. They told us that the only relief that they got in the frontlines was when we were over them or over the Germans in front of them. They said the Germans wouldn't shoot then for fear of giving their position away.

We talked and drank with them for some time — told them we'd better be going — couldn't stay out late at night — had to fly in the morning — and good luck to each of them. We had to shake hands with each man in that room again, and we left.

Sometime, after the fact, probably at Bad Kissinngen, Warren told me about his German messenger bike (motorcycle). It had large wheels, a powerful engine, and would just fly. He found a German that said he didn't want it any longer. Don't know what kind of persuasion Warren used, but Warren had a ball with that bike until — he was giving one of his buddies a ride around the taxi strip all around the field — and they were approaching a P-47 on a hard stand with its tail tied down and the engine turned up to about 2000 rpm. The tail was pointed toward the taxi strip. His buddy yelled, "Don't go through that prop blast." Warren yelled back, "No problem," and barreled right into the blast. The blast blew them off the taxi strip and down a bank. They ended up with the bike on top of them with the motor running wide open. Warren's leg was pinned against the exhaust pipe and burning like fire. He finally got the engine cut off, and they got the bike off of themselves.

They were bruised and skinned all over. Warren walked away from that bike and never looked back. He left it where it lay.

The push to the Rhine was well under way. With the exception of one or two, our missions were now on the other side of the Rhine. The water affected the cloud formation over the river. On some days when there was a general overcast, we would climb above the clouds and there would be this long snaky trough over the water — dark, but clear. By the bends in the trough we could tell what town was under us. On other days the land masses would be clear, but there would be a snaky cloud right over the water. All of this was very picturesque, but what was down below wasn't.

We started working around Dusseldorf and the area to the right side of the Ruhr. Flak was heavy everywhere. A lot of times we would make our passes at ground level because the flak was so heavy higher up. This, of course, brought us in range of pistols, rifles, and pom-pom guns. A pom-pom was four machine guns mounted two to the side of a seat — like a tractor seat. The gunner sitting in the seat could fire all four at the same time. He was able to swivel 360 degrees by using foot pedals, and he was able to raise or lower the guns quickly and easily — all movement must have been on roller bearings.

The Germans were good at setting up flak traps. They usually used trucks as bait. In the first trap I got caught in there were about 15 trucks on a side road that went into the main road at 90 degrees. On the other side of the main road paralleled a railroad track. I started my run low and into the sides of the trucks. I fired right on in close to the trucks and broke left — which was normal. As I started breaking, I saw a commotion on a rail boxcar — the top and sides collapsed to the ground. In the middle of the car was mounted a pom-pom. The gunner was firing at me head on. He never shut off. As I went over him, my left wing tip was just a few feet from the top of his guns. I looked him straight in the eyes. He followed me into him — swiveled 180 degrees and followed me away from him. A going-away shot is the easiest one there is. From the time he started firing, I never took my eyes off that gunner — four barrels of fire firing point blank into my face. He spun those guns around in an instant — never took his eye off the gun sight — never stopped firing. I thought, "Clever bastards." I was past him — eyes still glued. The son of a bitch was going to shoot me down. I made my move. I yanked my nose up and to the left like I was going to try to climb out

— immediately kicked right rudder and with my nose up skidded to the right toward the ground. I kicked left rudder and then my nose to the right — then up — a skid to the left — back down to the ground. I didn't give him a straight away shot. Every time I skidded, long streaks of fire shot past me — to a gunner — where I should have been. I was out of his range.

My heart had jarred my Adams apple again. My adrenal glands had kicked off so many times that now there was an ache — almost a pain — in my lower back — each time.

Another flak trap was on an autobahn along the Rhine. The highway divided, leaving a wooded island between them. We had heard on the radio that another squadron had gone down into the trap.

Sanders led our flight. My wingman had aborted. We could see trucks zipping along the island. Sanders said, "Red 2, stay with Red 3. I'm going down to take a look." He dropped to about 4,000ft., made a 180 degree turn — began to drop lower when I saw an ME 262, twin engine German jet gliding right toward Sanders. I yelled, "Red 1, jet closing in on you at 9:00 o'clock." I rammed the throttle quadrant forward — hit water injection and split essed as he went under me. I was closing fast — had him in my gun sight — he was too far away to fire — still closing — and then there were two puffs of black smoke from his engines. I began firing — hoping for a chance hit. I was moving on, but that jet went off and left me like I was standing still. He flew into a cloud bank. Sanders was catching up. We skirted the clouds for some time, hoping the jet would come back out.

We forgot about the flak trap and headed home.

The only other encounter I had with jets was when two of them glided into a position just off my right wing. The German pilot was grinning. I blasted my throttle and turned toward them. Puffs of black smoke and they were gone. I fired in their general direction.

Apparently, the Germans had put these jets in the air without any armament. They were just coming off the assembly line. Had the Germans got these jets in the air earlier — at the optimum time — they would have won WW II. Even after the Normandy Invasion — September for sure — and probably as late as the Bulge in December — they would have shot every plane we had out of the air. Our fighters — P-47, P-51 and P-38s — would have been sitting ducks. One flight — 4 jets — could have easily destroyed a whole group of P-47s — 75 planes — in short order. Just imagine what a squadron — 30 jets — could do. After our fighters were gone, all our bombers — medium and heavy — had no chance at all.

At the time of the Bulge a good number of the Panzer Divisions were still intact. With our air power gone, the supply lines to them could have been reestablished. The advance of our armored divisions would have been stopped. The jets — which burned kerosene instead of high octane gasoline — could have easily cut our supply lines. They could have pushed what was left of us — back into the sea.

With the western front gone, the jets could have concentrated on the Russian supply lines, and that would have been it. The side that controlled the air would win.

WW II was a war of fronts — front lines. That's where all the fire power was. Once there was a break in a line by either side, there was nothing behind the line to stop the advance — no reserve armies — practically nothing. That's the reason Gen. Patton went almost to the Rhine when he broke out of the beachhead and through the German front line. The Germans didn't stop Patton. He could have gone all the way to Berlin. He ran out of fuel.

That's the reason the Bulge was almost a success. They, too, ran out of fuel — not knowing that they were within a few hundred yards of our major fuel depot. Even if the Germans had reached Antwerp, Holland — our major supply port — they would only have extended the end for a period of time. We still controlled the air. We would take our toll. The jets could make the only difference. With the protection of the jets, the Germans could have made the first atomic bomb before we did. I often have thought how few jets it would have taken.

Missions were coming fast. The amount of damage we were causing was unbelievable. I never saw as many steam engines and rail cars in my life. They were ours. Our squadron destroyed 56 locomotives in one day. To count a locomotive destroyed, it had to be bombed — direct hits — or pulverized by strafing. It had to be ruined — out of action. Rail cars had to be the same way — either on fire or unusable. In our debriefing after a mission each pilot would report the number destroyed, and if not for sure — the number damaged. Other pilots, especially wingmen, were able to confirm destroyed or damaged.

We were strafing a large rail yard. Every track was full — 20 tracks wide. A tank car would blow up in a fiery ball. Box cars were burning everywhere.

Right down the middle of the yard was a Red Cross train — passenger cars with their tops painted white with a large Red Cross. We had avoided getting too close to it, and that's the reason it was there. We had finished and had backed off to look over our work when the flight leader asked if anyone had hit the hospital train. No one had. He said, "I'm not satisfied. They're trying to fool us. I'm going back down and give it a short burst." He went in low into the side about the middle of the train. The whole middle of the yard blew up. It was an ammunition train.

One of the prettiest sights I ever saw was another ammunition train. This time all box cars. Sanders was leading the squadron. The train was snaked up through some fields and around the side of a hill into a small village. Sanders went down and into the middle of the train. It blew with a mighty blast. Sanders broke sharp left, but his wingman, Walton, tried to miss but flew through the blast. Then a slow chain reaction set in on the train. On each side of the original blast there would be a delay and then the next box car would blow — another delay — then another car. The air was filled with white and black streaks and shells popping all over. Great hunks of cannon shells would come out of a car and bounce across the fields. What a sight to see.

Back at the airbase we all went over to look at Walton's plane. It was absolutely full of holes. The crew chief found all sorts of pieces of shells lodged in the plane. The biggest piece was about 7"x12" and from the curvature must have been part of a 16" shell.

We loved to hunt tanks. The Germans hid them in all kinds of places. The tanks had only one vulnerable place — underneath near the rear. That's where the engines were with no armor plate like the rest of the tank. When we would locate a tank, we would maneuver around so that our approach was directly behind the tank. We would fire at the dark place between the tracks. Our APIs would hit the ground and bounce up into the engine area, with all the oil and fuel lines as well as fuel tanks, one good spark — and that's all she wrote. The tank would burn up. We knew that when the tank got hot enough inside, the tank crew would be coming out the top of the tank. We waited on some of them.

The tank crews tried to get their tanks under something. I saw a large haystack out in a field, and there were tank tracks coming out of a village straight to the haystack. I tracked him just like I would a rabbit. He was there all right — covered over with hay almost to the ground. A short burst set the hay on fire. While waiting for the tank to start burning I spotted a messenger on his motorcycle racing full speed down a road toward a two-story building. Shooting at a moving target is a lot of fun. I got lined up on him just as he reached the building. I raked him and then pulled up to the building. I saw his body bounce up and hit the building just under the second story windows, made a couple more passes — riddled the building — set it on fire. I figured there must be a high ranking officer in there, because the messenger sure was hell bent to get to somebody. Made a pass back by the haystack, the tank was burning.

Following the tank tracks back to the village, we began searching for more tanks. Sure enough — one had rammed into the first floor of a two story building. His ass end was still sticking out. (Just) About all streets in towns and villages are narrow and this made it impossible to make a low enough pass to get the APIs under his rear end. The building was burning. Don't know if the tank did or not.

The Germans were getting better and better with their anti-aircraft guns. They were learning about deflection — how to lead their target. In the past, if a flight went in 1, 2, 3, 4, in a straight line, the Germans would fire at the first ship — the second, third, or fourth plane was more likely to be hit. Now the first ship had flak all around it. But, in the past, we had learned not to go in 1, 2, 3, 4. The element leader would vary his pass enough as not to be in line with 1 and 2.

I was the element leader. Bob Wagner, a replacement pilot with enough experience to know better, was my wingman. The flight started a pass on a rail yard in Essen. 1 and 2 headed in. The flak was awful heavy. I flew on ahead — kept 1 and 2 in sight — winged over to go down — and saw that stupid bastard Wagner following 1 and 2. I was furious. He had committed the unpardonable sin. He was a wingman. He left his leader. He didn't get hit on that pass, but he sure did later. I made up for both of us. It's a wonder I didn't burn my gun barrels out — anything over a 6 second burst (continuous could get the barrels so hot that the rifling in the barrels would — for a better word — melt). Rifling in a barrel spins a bullet so it will travel in a straight line. Once the rifling was gone — tracers are the only way we could tell — they would come out of the barrel end over end. Absolutely useless — I opened my guns early — the trajectory of the bullets was pinpointed at 1,100 feet. My choice. The impact at 1,100 ft. some have estimated — was equivalent to a tank running 40 mph hitting a solid concrete wall. I fired on in until

I barely skimmed the tops of the rail cars on my break.

I didn't know what to do with Wagner. He knew better. I thought about reporting him — or chewing his ass out. I did nothing. Ultimately, it kinda came down to every man for himself — for his survival. Piss on him.

Wagner and Simpkins were responsible for getting together our first reunion after 37 years. There were 22 of us made it to St. Louis — Wagner lived nearby. He and his wife were wonderful hosts — lovely people. Seeing Wagner again made me realize that I felt the same way as I did 37 years earlier. It made me realize something else. At the time I was probably getting close to the point of "burn out." Did I blow that incident all out of proportion?

Mike O'Reagan was leading the squadron on the north side of the Ruhr. We were on an "Armed Recce" — target of opportunity. At 6,000 ft. Mike was making gradual coordinated turns. The rest of us were edgy. Sure enough, the Germans hit the lead ship — Mike. He immediately jettisoned his canopy — they had clobbered him. As he bailed out of the cockpit he hit the tail section. He was in a free fall. His wing man lost sight of him. Everyone was looking for his parachute to open. There were some low clouds. Someone yelled, "I think I saw his chute open."

Mike's legs had hit the tail section. Both were broken. American doctors in a POW camp did the best they could for him. The Germans wouldn't give them anything to work with. After the war he went through several operations. Both legs look shorter, and he walks with the slightest limp.

Schaefer was leading our flight. I was the element leader. At our briefing a weather Recce pilot had reported some heavy clouds along the Rhine. But beyond over the Ruhr was mostly clear. We could see the clouds ahead of us. We began to climb. At 10,000 ft. we began to hit the tops of some of them. I had already set my gyro instruments. I began to close in on Schaefer. All at once we were in a solid cloud. Schaefer disappeared. I kept trying to find him — to move closer to him. Without my eyes on the gyro flight indicator, I got vertigo. My gyro instruments were tilted. My altimeter was spinning downward — 9,000, 8,000, 7,000. All I had left to get the plane righted was the needle and ball. I'd get the ball centered and the needle would be all the way to one side. I'd bring the needle to center, and the ball would be to one side. I had no idea what my attitude was. I even suspected I was on my back. At 5,000 ft. I called Schaefer — told him I was probably in a flat spin and that I was going to bail out soon. He yelled, "Go on needle and ball — needle and ball." I thought, "What does that son of a bitch think I've been trying to do?" At 4,000 ft. I came into a shaft of light to the ground almost sideways — righted my wings — caged and uncaged the gyro flight indicator back in the clouds — made a 360 degree turn — came back into the shaft of light — reset my instruments — got on the original heading — and started climbing. I broke out on top at 12,600 ft. There were clouds as far as I could see on that 90 degree heading. (The weather Recce pilot must have made his forecast from his sack.)

I called Jampit. No answer. Finally I called Rosalee; they thought my squadron was on ahead. Call again, in about 10 minutes. After talking to Rosalee the next time, I flew out of their range. I knew I was deep into Germany. There was nothing on the radio — dead silence. Figuring my gas supply, I turned back. After sometime I heard Jampit on the radio. Rosalee got me back with them. They were hunting a target on the north side of the Ruhr — the clouds were partly broken. I was about 2,000 ft. above them, and as I dived and came in from the rear a plane with a different tail color in one flight peeled away and into a cloud. "That's odd," I said to myself. "If that was a plane that was lost from another squadron, he wouldn't have left." Bingo! That was a German just waiting for some action to start so he could shoot down the other 3 in the flight. The odds were good that I was right.

Another mission with Schaefer — we were at 6,000 ft. just over the Rhine hunting a juicy target. After several turns we were headed back toward the Rhine. I said, "Jampit White 1, box of bombers high at 9:00 o'clock." They were at 12,000 — about 20 medium bombers — coming straight down the Rhine. Schaefer kept heading right on under them. Their bombs were away — a whole cloud of them. I was on Schaefer's right — well to the side and some below him. We and the bombs were going to meet. Schaefer suddenly broke down and right. I was breaking too, but I heard his engine go by me awful close. When we got home the top of my rudder — about 12" — was bent over to the right at 90 degrees. We walked over to Schaefer's plane, and there was a slight dent with blue paint on it under his engine cowling just behind the propeller. His prop had passed in front of my rudder. The prop should have reached my fuselage, but didn't. Correction — he bent over my vertical stabilizer. The rudder is the movable part of that air surface.

HOWARD I. "HI" PRICE

Bless his heart. He was coming up off a strafing pass — took a direct hit almost under his cockpit — his auxiliary tank burst into flames — he held his altitude for a few seconds and then started toward the ground. "GET OUT! GET OUT! Leave it Price." He jettisoned his canopy. He was almost into the ground. He stood up with his back up in the slipstream and pulled his rip cord. The chute jerked him out of the cockpit. He oscillated back and forward one time and hit the ground. His plane crashed a short distance in front of him. He was on his back. About 30 ft. away was a startled German farmer, who had been hoeing in his field. The farmer raised the hoe over his head and charged toward Price. Price was still strapped into his chute — he unbuckled both leg straps and his chest strap and rolled over just as the farmer came down with his hoe — he missed. Price scrambled up and ran for his life — the farmer whacking right behind him. Price jumped over a hedge row — looked back — the farmer had stopped.

Price scrunched over and ran along the hedgerow. He heard rifle shots. He came to another hedgerow that crossed his and took off down it. In the distance and down a hill he saw a building. There was a man standing in the doorway motioning for Price to come to him. Price thought — Oh, Boy — he's going to hide me and take care of me. He ran like a blue streak — right on through the doorway into the building. The man closed the door behind Price, and behind the door was a German soldier with a Mauser pointed right between Price's eyes.

He was taken to the company headquarters and put in a room by himself. After a while, a German Lt. and three others came in and very nicely started asking questions. Price answered each with rank, name and serial number, "Lt. Price, Howard I, 0-7 — — ."

They pulled out their pistols and talked rougher than hell to Price. Price said he knew his number was up — that they were going to kill him. Even though he was scared to death, he tried his best not to show it. They left.

Every little bit the German Lt. would come back in the room — get right up in Price's face and say, "Kaput," and then just die laughing.

The next morning Price and 12 more prisoners were started walking down a road. After a couple of miles a German staff car came whizzing by —

screeched to a halt — backed up — a staff officer got out and headed for Price — the only officer. In good English the staff officer jerked Price to attention and proceeded to dress him down because his men weren't in a military formation. Price saluted him — turned to the other prisoners and said, "Fall in — two abreast. Attention — forward march — hut, two, three, four." Down the road they went, and Price was singing out.

After four days of reaching a German outfit and being sent to another, Price ended up with the same Germans that had captured him. They were now in a railroad tunnel. The same German Lt. came up to Price and started the "Kaput" and laughing again. Price got his nerve up and told him, "Look, you are my prisoner. I'm not your prisoner. You're surrounded." The Lt. studied Price for a minute — turned and left. About 3 hours later he came back and wanted to know what Price's terms of surrender were. Price said, "First, give up all your arms. I'll leave 8 of my men here to guard your troops. You and three more that I will pick will go down the railroad track until we make contact with an American unit, and then we'll come back with them to get the rest of these people."

About an hour later all the German officers came — lined up in front of Price — came to attention, and the Lt. said, "We accept your terms of surrender."

Price and the 8 others headed down the track. After about 2 miles two Germans with their hands up climbed onto the track ahead of them. The four Germans with Price dived into the ditch along the railroad. Price walked on ahead by himself — stopped — and said, "Advance and be recognized." The two were SS Troopers. They wanted to surrender. Price disarmed them, and ordered the others to join up.

Price could hear gunfire — some of it pretty close. He'd stop — wait a minute — and proceed. They came to the edge of a little town. Price told the rest of them to stay put, and he would go ahead and make contact. He said — advancing step by step — that the first thing he was aware of was part of a helmet sticking out from a corner of a building with an eye looking down an M-1 rifle pointed straight at him. He threw up his hands — gave his rank — name — and serial number. "Stand still," a voice said. Another person stepped out into the open. "C'mere," he said.

Price was taken to a Lt., who sent a couple of squads back with him. Price was responsible for capturing 282 Germans. He was riding high. He had probably done something no one else had. But the captain sent for him — the company commander. He chewed Price's butt out until it wouldn't hold shucks. "What in the hell do you mean bringing in SS troopers alive?" And so on —

When Price got back to us, he was loaded with German items — beautiful leather boots — Lugers — and the like — some of which the German officers gave him.

An omen! 38th mission. A rifle bullet passed through my right wing. The first time I had been hit.

Lloyd G. Cotsenmoyer was my wingman. I was on my 41st mission. He was on his 2nd with me. We were strafing near Essen. I came up off a pass and was almost at the top looking back and down for the next target. My nose was still a little up — the leftwing down about 30 degrees. There was a Bump-Clank. I had been hit — not from a gun under me, but a deflection shot from some distance away. About 3 ft. from the cockpit was a hole in my left wing that I could have jumped through with my elbows spread. My left wing went under and my nose straight down. I blasted my throttle — my nose came up about to level — the left wing went down and my nose down. What went through my mind was, "God dammit, this is it." I was shocked at the thought. I had always been a fairly religious person, and now I had taken his name in vain. The left aileron cable was cut. I was cork-screwing down — nose up — leftwing under — nose down. At this point I had only one chance, and that was to hit the ground while I was pulling my nose up. I was working on how to make this happen. I couldn't bail out. The movements of the plane were extremely violent. I couldn't turn loose of the controls or I would have nosed straight into the ground.

That old baby doll shuddered — and again. My engine was wide open and wound up. That ole big four-bladed prop was doing its thing. I was hung on it. My right rudder was jammed all the way in. This had the rudder on the tail section almost 90 degrees to the right, and it was keeping the tail down. My stick was all the way to the right but close to neutral. The left wing was down about 30 degrees. The right wing was up and blanking out the airflow to the right aileron — which was turned all the way up. It would appear that I was making a climbing turn to the left. But, actually I was skidding almost belly first to the right about 30 degrees.

When I got hit, I was on a 90 degree heading — right into Germany. When I quit cork-screwing, I was headed toward the Rhine — a 270 degree heading. From 90 degrees to 270 degrees, I had done everything humanly possible to make the plane fly, but I was absolutely helpless when it came to the direction it would fly. A feeling of instant peace shot through me. It hadn't been my time. The odds were just too great that by chance I ended up on that 270 degree heading. Inside me said, "Thanks."

I had to get us down — me and my noble airplane. My canopy was slicked over with oil — hydraulic or engine or both, I couldn't see. I thought I'll fix that. I pulled my goggles down and slid my canopy back. Immediately my goggles oiled over. I pushed them back up. The slipstream was coming almost sideways through the cockpit, with a terrible roar. My eyes smarted — or rather, burned like hell.

I was gathering myself. All my pitot tube, static pressure instruments were gone. I needed to know what my airspeed was. I closed the canopy and called Cotsie. "About 160 mph," he said. I asked Cotsie to do something that in retrospect I probably shouldn't have, "Cotsie, if you see any of those sons of bitches shooting at me — shoot back at them." He could have stayed up higher and taken evasive action. Instead, when the clouds of flak started popping, I would see him on my right

— nose down — and he'd come up on my left — nose down — and back up on my right — time after time. He was blasting me a path through two Panzer Divisions (Harings told me later). With my skidding to the right, most of the flak was on my left. I was only 500 ft. high — in rifle range — much less the cannons. They began to feel for me. I could see some blasts getting close. I heard two more Bump-Clanks — figured the tail or fuselage got hit.

We got to the Rhine. Cotsie went down once more. He said later that he strafed a barge. He said, "You tried your best to tell me about flak and how to evade it, but I thought you were exaggerating. When I strafed that barge, I was shaking so bad that my feet were bouncing on the rudders. I nearly flew into the opposite bank."

Past the Rhine everything got quiet. "Son," I said to my plane, "I've got to get us down." I closed the canopy and asked Cotsie what was ahead of me. He described fields that one normally would [where one could land], but I couldn't maneuver the plane. I had tried. I cut the throttle back ever so little — the left wing started on under. Next, I tried moving my stick forward a little while pumping the rudder. I was able to push the nose to the right a degree or two.

My gas gauge had been falling like the Titanic. I had to get down. I had to see what was ahead of me. Finally I raised my seat until I could get a glimpse through the "V" formed between the right wing and fuselage. I saw a pine field. How long does it take one to think — to solve a problem? Believe me — quicker than an instant. I knew what I had to do — lower my nose so that the right aileron would have more effect — my nose would come to the right. I knew when I started pulling the nose back up that the left wing would start under. I had already figured if I tried to land in a field that the left wing would hit first and I would cartwheel across the ground. Now I had a cushion. I wanted that left wing to start hitting the tops of the pines so the pines would knock the wing up. I would then pitch into the pines about level.

That's what happened. My plan worked to perfection. I had kept my nose pointed down as long as possible, the throttle still wide open. I had to be going a minimum of 200 mph. I started the nose up — the left wing began hitting the pines and came up. I jerked the throttle off and plunged down into the pines at about 45 degrees. Johns asked me later if I had gone in sideways, I said, "Not quite."

After the initial lunge in the pines I was thrown back left and then to the right again — that's when the right wing broke off. When the wing went off, the right aileron cable jerked the stick out of my hand, and it hit my left leg on the side of the shinbone. With both wings gone, the engine and cockpit — that's all that was left — continued on ahead. I had one more plan — I was going to get away from the plane as fast as I could before it blew up.

We came to a stop. I had gone in with my canopy open — on purpose. The cockpit was filled with debris — dirt — pine needles, limbs. The first thing I did was to run my left hand through that stuff and cut the main switch — pure training — the last thing you do before crash landing. Worthless now, but I didn't have time to get to it before. Next, I took both arms and threw all the shit I could out the top of the cockpit — came back with my right hand — hit the safety belt buckle — threaded both arms under the safety straps — came up out of the cockpit and over the side — picked a path in the pines — put my head down and charged like a full back — in a straight line. After about 15 or 20 steps I ran out of air and hit the ground. The shoulder straps had jerked my breath out. Naturally, I hadn't been able to keep my mouth shut and it was full of junk. I ran my pointing finger into my mouth back toward my throat and raked a big glob out so I could get a breath.

I got to my knees — turned my head and looked back — what was left of the plane was burning, smoke about 50 feet high. Earlier, when I'd close my canopy, the cockpit would fill up with smoke. I had a fire somewhere. I still didn't feel that I was a safe distance from the plane. I picked a path — put my head down and charged again. When I ran out of air again — I stopped — looked back. Black smoke was now about 100 feet in the air.

Cotsie came swooping over me. I thought he was going to hit the pines. I walked on out into a clearing and farther on to the edge of a sloping bank. Cotsie made another pass — I waved — but don't think he saw me — and he left.

I sat down on top of the bank with my feet resting below me. I took my parachute off — about 4 ft. was dangling from the top right corner. I thought, what if the chute had been jerked on out of the pack and hung on something? My helmet, goggles, and oxygen mask had been swept away. My face was stinging all over — felt like it was raw. I looked down and the zipper on my flight jacket about 6" down on the right side was torn in two. My left leg began to hurt. I felt a quiver of the shakes.

There was a small town in the distance. A small boy about 10 or 12 years old was pedaling toward me on a bicycle. We couldn't understand one another, but I made him understand to go to the town and bring the military police. I would make out like I had a cap on with a visor — brim on it. I'd take the brim between my thumb and first finger and shake it. Then I would wrap my fingers around my left arm, like a band was on it — all the time saying, "Police — military police," and I'd point to the town. "Ya, Ya, Ya," and he took off. I saw 10 or 12 other children his age running toward me. Some could speak some English. They hesitated just long enough to find out I was the only one in the plane, and then took off running into the pines toward the plane. I yelled for them to stop — the plane was going to blow up. They paid me no mind. I realized the little bastards were scavengers.

Then there were about 10 old people walked up to me. As they approached, I didn't like their looks — mean looking people — with long coats on. I didn't trust them. I thought that after what I had just been through I wasn't going to let them hit me in the head without a fight. I swiveled a little to the right — unsnapped my holster — took the safety off my .45 pistol and loosened it in the holster. We couldn't understand one another. Sounded like they were speaking Dutch — didn't sound like

Flemish. They wanted to know by gestures if I was the only one in the plane. I would point to myself and nod yes. Then I tried to tell them that those children were going to get hurt and should come away from the plane. It was hopeless. I was only confusing them.

I got my cigarettes out and took one out of the pack and handed the pack to a man closest to me. They passed the pack one to another — each taking one cigarette — the last man passing the pack back to me. I lit mine. They didn't — carefully putting them in their pockets. I was stalling for time. I remembered the G.I. chocolate in a pocket of my flying suit — got it out — passed it to them. It was hard to break. They kept all of it.

A British soldier came running up. I took him to be a Corporal. He saluted. I returned — told him I was the only one in the plane — but that those children were in there and were going to get hurt and would he please get them out of there. "Yessah," he said, and saluted and started. I said, "Corporal, stay with that plane until you're relieved." Each pilot that crash landed was to stay with his plane until relieved. Those were my orders. My feelings were hurt. I wasn't going to stay with the damned thing.

I began studying those people closer. Their faces were wrinkled and weather worn. Their eyes had a glazed look to them; they were grim looking. Lord, what those people must have been through the last four years.

I saw a jeep with an ambulance coming across the fields. Every now and then they would dodge big holes in the ground — more like craters — and probably caused by artillery shells sometime in the past. They stopped about 30 yards from me. A British officer got out of the jeep — by his insignia I decided he must be a Major. He walked up to me. I made no effort to try to get up. He climbed part of the way up the bank — put his hands on his left knee — and peered intently into my face. Then we went through that I was the only one in the plane, etc. I got to my feet, and he helped me down the bank, and I walked the rest of the way to the jeep. He had asked if I wanted to ride in the ambulance or the jeep. I said, "Awh, I'll ride in the jeep." I turned and sat in the seat and after 3 or 4 tries, I couldn't get my feet high enough to get them inside. The major's sergeant, the driver, ran around to me — took hold of my ankles and twisted me into the jeep.

The sergeant sat me down into a blond oak desk type chair, with arms on it, with my back to the long wall — the map wall of the major's office. I didn't trust the major and his sergeant. Somehow, I had a feeling that I had been — well — captured.

The major said something to the sergeant that I couldn't hear. The sergeant opened a door at my right elbow and as he passed through I made a quick glance down a hallway.

The shakes had me now. I'd take a deep breath — hold it — the shakes would hesitate — I'd exhale — and shake again. The major was reading and shuffling papers at his desk — in silence. He'd slip a glance at me — now and then. The sergeant, after what seemed a long time, came back through the door. He handed me a mug of the hottest, blackest tea I ever saw. Yes, I said to myself. I've arrived after their tea time. I curled my lip back and sipped. The mug was shaking in my hand. I used both hands and that helped. I could feel my insides getting hot all the way to the bottom of my stomach. That tea was the best stuff I ever tasted in my life. I could feel it working; by the time I emptied the mug, my shakes were gone.

The sergeant was seated on his side of the major's desk. They both watched while I drank the tea. When the shakes were gone, the major came over and asked me where my airfield was. I couldn't tell him that. Our strip was secret. My orders were not to tell anyone. I got up — found Zwartberg — made a pretty large circle and told him that it was in that area. He said, "Lt. — after studying a minute — you can spend the night with us — we'll contact your outfit, and they can pick you up in the morning." I must have made a bad reaction. "Or," he said, "I'll give you a jeep and driver now." I answered, "Major, if you would give me a jeep and driver, I would thank you from the bottom of my heart." He smiled.

I was helped into a jeep and the driver and I took off. The field was about 40 miles away. The driver had been in several campaigns — North Africa, 2 or 3 — Normandy — and others. When we arrived, I tried my best to get him to come in and have a cup of coffee. "No sir," he said, "My orders are to deliver you and return." He helped me out of the jeep. I watched him drive away. It suddenly dawned on me that I hadn't had enough sense to get the major's name or address — so I could thank him.

I walked into operations. There were 3 or 4 people in there. There was a big-eyed peculiar look on their faces. I thought, "What the hell is going on?" One of them ran out the door. The others finally rushed up to me with, "Lt. we sure didn't expect to see you! Where did you come from? How did you get here?" Some of the pilots came bursting through the door — some hugged me — some patted me — one let out a war whoop — and everyone was laughing and even shaking hands with one another. I didn't know quite what to make of all the to-do — really didn't care because I was home — no finer place to be in the whole world — Oh! Home!

It turned out that Doc Milligan, his sergeant, and Johns had gone in the ambulance to the crash site to pick me up. I found out much later that actually they had gone to pick up my body. Everyone at home thought I was KIA [killed in action].

Someone had immediately called the group surgeon. He came in short order — took me into an adjoining room, the officer's mess — had people to help me get my clothes off — and stretched me, stark naked, out on one of the wooden tables that we ate on. After he had examined me, someone handed me a four-finger glass of bourbon, and I was taken to the infirmary and put to bed.

I remember very few things of the next few weeks. It was as if my mind went blank.

My left leg looked terrible — greatly swollen from the knee down. The foot was about 3" thick. The leg and foot were all kinds of colors — blue, black, yellow, green, purple and violet. With my index finger I would mash any part of the leg, and the imprint would stay there a long time before it dissipated. I used crutches to get to a room where Doc's sergeant would put my foot in a bucket of hot water and wrap hot towels around my leg.

Serving Their Country

Stars A

Purple Heart Medals Awarded 6 From WNC

Purple Heart medals for wounds received in action have been awarded six Western North Carolina servicemen. They are:

First. Lt. Herschel D. Ponder, 23, son of Mr. and Mrs. O. W. Ponder of Skyland; at a ninth air force fighter - bomber base in Germany, for wounds received while piloting his P-47 over enemy territory heavily defended by flak.

PONDER

I remember seeing children going through the garbage cans outside our mess tent — now and then, an old person waiting at a distance.

I missed Mayer and Johns. They also were getting ahead of me in missions. When the swelling started down, I asked Doc to let me fly. He said, "Later." The next time I asked, he said, "You're not ready yet. I'll let you know." He probably thought more than my leg got hurt, and I suppose that I was in some kind of a state of shock. I did realize that the experience had taken a whole lot out of me.

While I was grounded, Mayer and Johns flew about 15 missions. By the end of the war each had flown around 65 missions.

The Purple Heart

Mayer and I and four other pilots were given a 7-day R&R (rest and recuperation) to Cannes. We stayed at the hotel Martinique, which had been a swanky place. Mayer and I had a delightful room with twin beds — soft easy chairs on each side of a table — and a bath that wouldn't quit. The floor and walls were all ceramic tiled, and the john was in a cubicle all by itself.

We ate in the main dining room that had waiters to serve us. The French cooks could make the G.I. food much more palatable. Each evening Mayer and I would sit at a table for two and order a bottle of wine to go with our meal. Off the rear of the main lobby was a bar. In addition to all the usual, they also had Coca Colas. The first we'd had overseas. Boy! They were good. We even got to putting bourbon in the cokes.

Mayer and I were not heavy drinkers. So we ended up putting the other four to bed for 6 nights straight. On the afternoon of the seventh day Mayer said, "You do remember that we brought a fifth of Johnny Walker Red Label scotch with us? Let's don't carry it back home." In mid-afternoon we started sipping scotch while sitting in those easy chairs and talking. On toward supper time we decided to go by the bar on the way to the dining room — coke and bourbon. We had our usual bottle of wine with our meal. After eating we went back to the bar. There were a bunch of rowdies in there. Someone said we'd better quiet down before the MPs came and got us — there were some always stationed in the lobby. A voice said, "Let's go down to the dock area where the night life is." "Away we go," in unison.

In the lobby I remembered the scotch — about $1/3$ of the bottle left. I said, "Wait a minute" to Carnduff, and charged up the stairs — got the scotch — hid it under my jacket (no public drinking — only the bar) and raced back down stairs. I showed Carnduff what I had — he took it from me — screwed the cap off — and took a big swig — and handed it to Bremseth, his buddy.

Outside it was black as pitch. We turned right and started walking. After a ways a young lady came by riding a bicycle. I took off running to catch her. I was no match. Out of breath, I stopped — Carnduff came running up to me. He still had the bottle of scotch. We both had a swig. We called for Mayer and Bremseth — no answer. "Well, we'll just have to find them." We made it down to the café district — a café every other door it seemed. Carnduff and I would go in — look around — and sit at a table. We felt obligated to buy a drink — which was a watery tasting French beer. We'd go to the next café and the next — and finally we went into one — sat at a table across from the bar — about 10 ft. away — and I ordered an orangeade. I looked toward the bar, but I couldn't see it. I knew it was there because I could hear voices behind it. I told Carnduff that we had to get out of there. Out on the sidewalk, I was sicker than hell and started up-chucking. It helped my vision, if I would close one eye. We discussed which way was home. I said, "Well we can't end up on the beach where we see all those German prisoners sapping mines. Follow me," I said. I picked out a street. Soon we were climbing. Carnduff argued that we were going the wrong way. "A few more blocks," I said. "No not this one — not this one — here's where we turn right," I said. Down-hill 2-½ blocks we hit the main drag. I stood there and studied, "We go right." In the middle of that block was the hotel.

Just before we got to the lobby, I told Carnduff to hold his head up and walk straight and make a bee-line for the stairs. We didn't want those damned MPs to get us.

Carnduff opened the door. I walked in, and on my right in the bathroom was Mayer — stark naked with a blanket wrapped around his shoulders — Bremseth had brought him in earlier — standing in front of the wash basin. Carnduff helped me get my clothes off and into bed — and left. The bed was rolling over and over. Mayer heaved. We had both already lost everything in our stomachs, including the green stuff. I ran to the john. First, I'd heave and that would start Mayer. He would and then I would. I'd lean over the commode and "Bang" my head would hit the tile wall behind it. So I tried not to hit my head straight away; it would go "Bang" on one side or the other. There was nothing to hold to.

At a pause we both made a dash to the beds. I made a mistake. I closed my eyes, and there was all kinds of whirling and shooting lights. Up I went again — Mayer followed. We tried the beds again. This time I kept my eyes open and put my head under the pillow so I couldn't hear.

The next morning we were miserable, and if there's anything worse than miserable, we were that too. We dressed. We had to go home. On the way down the steps we stopped off at the infirmary. The nurse was nice enough to not grin. The doctor just died laughing — gave us both a tall glass of white liquid — and told us to keep stirring and drinking until it was all gone. He wasn't much of a doctor — didn't make us feel better — maybe a little.

We flew out of Cannes to Marseille to gas up. When we climbed out of the plane, Mayer waited on the pilot, and I heard him say, "Say Bud, can't you take us up a little higher where it won't be so rough?"

We landed at Orly in Paris. In the transient center we ate our supper — the first food we had eaten all day — and then went straight to bed — I in the top bunk — Mayer in the bottom. It wasn't even dark yet.

Back at Y-32 someone said I needed a check ride — not having flown for some time. A crew chief had been working on the water injection system. He needed it tested. I had a peculiar sensation when I sat down in the cockpit. I had an urge to climb back out. When I got airborne, I headed out on the edge of the British restricted zone — got altitude — shoved everything forward — bypassed the throttle stop and clicked the switch on top of the throttle. I was pulling about 40" of mercury and it went to 60" where it was supposed to stop. I clicked the switch off — the power continued to climb to 90". The engine was supposed to have blown up, but it didn't. This gauge with a column of mercury in it was on the instrument panel and showed the power output of the engine at any given setting of the throttle. The power developed on take-off was about 50 inches on the mercury scale. The gauge took its reading from the intake manifold of the engine and was red lined at 60". The engine was in danger of blowing up with any reading much over 60."

The target at my first briefing back was a German airfield, and their fields were notorious about air defense. I thought, "Lord, not again this quick." The field was full of fighters — JU88's — And Heinkel 111 bombers. We had a goodly number burning when we left — but OH! That flak. It was awful — just indescribable.

Carnduff got hit strafing an airfield near Hanover — two of his eighteen cylinders were shot out. His engine was rough and shaking the plane — and would miss and Carnduff kept yelling that it was going to quit — all the time getting closer to home — and he made it. Hanover was nearly two hours from our field. A crippled engine can't fly that long — but it did.

Then we started flying missions all the way to Magdeburg, which was way beyond our range. To get there, we carried a big belly gas tank. When we got there, we would drop the belly tank before making our bomb run with two 500 pounders. Then we'd do our strafing. We had the whole area for miles burning. The smoke was very thick and went up to 10,000 ft. On the way home we dropped into a grass strip to get enough fuel to make it the rest of the way. The strip was on the north side of the Ruhr, and our trucks were there with the gas.

Those long missions like to have killed me. I would ache all over. My legs would get numb — my butt would get prickly. I'd put my left hand under my left cheek then swap to the right. I'd grasp a knee with both hands and pull my leg back far enough to put my foot on the instrument panel. I did most of the flying with trim tabs — hardly ever touched the controls. The plane was so sensitive to my weight that every time I moved I'd have to reset the tabs.

By the time I'd get to the grass strip, I would be so despondent that I didn't care much whether I landed or not. I would point the nose toward the field and flop or bounce all over the place — sometimes hot as a pistol. I'd unlock my tail wheel about half way down the strip and at about 40 mph make my turn toward the trucks — stop — cut the engine — and raise my seat as high as it would go. I would be almost standing up. We didn't get out of the plane. But standing up helped my legs. One time I unbuckled my seat belt and shoulder straps and peed over the side of the plane. The planes were equipped with relief tubes — a rubber cup of a thing with a small hose long enough to reach with the seat partly raised. The tube ran to the outside of the plane. After I got my own plane, I didn't use mine because of the smell.

The gas trucks didn't take long. We only got about 100 gallons apiece. Roaring down to the end of the strip — one of the gas trucks had a wind sock on top of it — we'd make a fast turn — lock our tail wheels, and we were gone from there.

MAJ. HARRY SANDERS,
OPERATIONS OFFICER

Sandy had been operations officer the whole time I had been in the squadron until now. He was pulling a Knisley — flying almost every mission. He, too, was burning out. Like Knisley, he was an excellent pilot and very aggressive on his missions.

Sandy led the squadron to Magdeburg. The river that ran through Magdeburg was as far as we could advance. Roosevelt, Stalin and Churchill had had a meeting and decided that was as far as we could go. Somehow we all felt cheated. We were almost to Berlin, which was only a short distance away. Some of our missions at Magdeburg could have been spent in Berlin. The sky over Magdeburg was filled with thick haze and smoke. On a strafing pass Sandy misjudged and flew into the ground. Unbelievable! Someone else maybe — but not Sanders. At a speed of minimum 300 mph he went through the corner of a brick building — then through some trees. All that got through the trees into a field was the cockpit, and it was rolling side over side. Sandy's wingman had followed him through all of this and reported that when the cockpit came to rest he did not see any movement. Sandy was gone. Sandy had been killed.

We all knew that no one could survive a crash like that, but Sandy did. He was taken prisoner. His injuries consisted of the bulb of his nose, which was all but cut off, and some lacerations on one arm. The Germans in the prison camp wouldn't give the American doctors the supplies necessary to sew the bulb back on. The doctors told Sandy that the only thing to do was hold the bulb in place with his finger — and it knitted back — but left a terrible scar.

On May 8, 1945, we were on an airfield R-6 in Bad Kitzengen, Germany, and Sandy called us to come and get him. Sandy was alive! We whooped and hollered. He had come back from the dead!

One of the pilots jumped in a P-47 piggyback — one with an added seat — and brought him home. All of us went to the flight line to meet him. As he approached, Donovan took one look — got down on his knees — raised his arms overhead and bowed to the pavement several times — stood up — pointed to Sanders's nose and said, "You damned son of a bitch, don't you ever call me 'droop snoop' again." Donovan had a hawkish nose, and Sanders kidded him a lot about it. Both had tears in their eyes — the rest of us did too.

We strafed one airfield for fighters only — ME 109s, FW 190s, and long-nose 190s. Talk about clever. My goodness. An autobahn made a curve near a wooded area. The side next to the woods was used as a runway. The taxi strips into the woods were covered with camouflage materials making the entrance look like a dark hole. I thought of a hornet's nest — the fighters shooting out of the hole at top speed.

The flak in that area was murderously heavy.

The thing that got our attention to this curve was that there were no posts in the median of the autobahn. The posts kept gliders from landing there. We moved to Bad Kitzengen. The hanger on the former German airfield was burned out except for the office building on one end. The Germans were almost defeated.

Next to the wall of the office part, Warren's C.O. put his mobile office for Warren to use as a radio shop for all three squadrons. If you came into possession of a radio that wouldn't play, that's where you took it. When you climbed into the trailer, you'd most likely find Warren with his feet up on the desk — leaned back in a very comfortable chair — fiddling with a radio's innards. He and I both knew we had done the best job — through hell and high water — that we could do. I sure was proud of him.

I thought of a time early on when he told me about his C.O. asking, "Trantham, can you run a movie projector?" "Yes sir," Warren answered. To me he said that the closest he'd been to one was to watch — at a distance — someone thread the film through the slots and turn the projector on. His motto had always been (as well as all the Tranthams) "If anybody else can do it, I can do it too." He set the projector up and focused it on the screen — put the return reel on — the film reel on top — threaded the film, and said, "Lights Out." The first reel ran beautifully. The second was terrible. The whole squadron hooted and hollered at him. Under all that pressure he finally figured out that whoever had used the second reel last hadn't rewound it. After the movie some of his buddies came by and said, "Great job, Bird Ass."

Jenkins led the squadron. I was White Flight leader. We saw the shadow of a plane on the ground. At first we couldn't see the plane. It was camouflaged. Jenks said, "He's mine. The rest of you stay up here." He winged over — went to the deck — and shot down a twin engine aircraft.

Another day we caught a passenger train balling the jack toward a town in the distance. The engineer had the engine really bird-working. The whole squadron made one pass. Every car was crammed with people — mostly military. When I went in, they were jumping out of windows and doorways. I cut my blasts short. Donovan said later that just as he fired, a bunch of people were crowding down the steps, and his blasts knocked them back up into the vestibule.

My last mission was to Linz. The flak was unbelievable — the last time I ever saw man made clouds.

I got word that on Saturday about 1:00 p.m., there was going to be some good music on the radio in communications. There were 12 of us. I was the only officer. It started DaDaDa Da___ Beethoven's 5th Symphony. Every cell in my body seemed to tingle. My hair must have been standing straight up. Good Lord! What music! It had been years. I tried to wipe my eyes with the back of my hands. I was embarrassed to be so emotional — until I saw some others reach for their handkerchiefs. Then — I did too.

During the week ending May 8th, several German officers flew light planes into our field and surrendered — some with their families. One of the planes was a "stork," a high winged odd looking thing. A high ranking German officer climbed out of one of the planes and started barking orders. Our officer of the day that met him listened for a minute and then said, "Hold it, Buddy. You've already said too much. You're not in the German army anymore, and if there's any damn orders to be issued around here, I'll do it."

Nothing. Nothing to do — no missions to fly — no more bombing runs — no more strafing — no more destruction. The relief and exhilaration of a dog fight was gone. No more briefings — and debriefings. No more front lines — or flak maps. No more flak — thank God — no more flak.

There was an emptiness — a void. All my life — until now — I was always in school or training for something. I would have never dreamed that my ultimate job would be death and destruction. Dammit! I was good. I was a professional. Few men in the whole world could have done any better. I tabbed myself as a "professional exterminator."

And now it was over. My job was finished — and I had survived. Surviving had taken everything I was made of — mental capacity — nervous system — stamina — courage — grit — tenacity — and heart — and probably the most important of all — the ability to concentrate — one lapse and blooie.

Each mission had taken its toll. I operated at 100% of what was in me, and there seemed to be less and less in me — particularly after about my 35th mission. I noticed that barrel chested men seemed to have more stamina — get up and go — lasted longer. But when they broke, they were done for — no nervous system left. The thin ones didn't have the pep but seemed never to quite wear out — at least visibly. After my 51st mission when everything came to a sudden halt, I realized that I had used up most of what there was.

I felt I was more and more alone — that the weight of the world was pressing in on me. I was through — had had enough. No one else seemed to notice.

Mayer must have felt somewhat the same way. He said, "Lick, let's get some exercise before we both fall flat on our faces. Let's go take a look at the woods (Germans called them forests) north of the field." The woods were just beautiful — no undergrowth — the floor was almost like a carpet. The Germans didn't waste anything — not a twig or blade of grass.

I saw two squirrels about 50 yards ahead of us jumping from tree to tree trying to get away from us. I said, "C'mon Mayer, let's run and get under them." They were large and had big ears and were a reddish brown. Mayer took one and I took the other. Mine tried to hide on a limb near the top of a tree. I looked him out — pulled my .45 — took good aim — and pulled the trigger. I must have missed by a mile, but the noise made him take off again. Every time he stopped — I fired until my pistol was empty — put in another clip — and started firing again. I could hear Mayer blasting away. I finally lost mine. He had to be in the tree I was under. I walked around the tree 3 or 4 times and finally got a glimpse of him about 25 feet up and on the trunk of the tree. He had been taking the back side on me. I eased up to the trunk and leaned my head around. There he was flat against the trunk. I aimed — holding my hand against the trunk to steady my pistol and fired straight up the tree. All kinds of bark and grumlins fell in my face. That squirrel sure enough took off that time, and I had had enough.

I told Mayer that if we came back, we'd bring a carbine. We sure couldn't hunt squirrels with a .45 Colt pistol.

Our next move was to Straubing. The field had been used by the Germans, and all the buildings were still intact. The Danube River generally flowed northeast out of the Alps to Regensburg where it made a sharp turn to the southeast — and on into Austria. We were not too far from the Austrian border.

Our group CO was a pretty smart cookie. He figured out the quickest and easiest way to move the personnel from Kitzengen to Straubing. In looking through the files of pilots, he found that Johns had flown twin engine planes back in the states. He had ordered a C-47 transport that was sitting on the flight line. He told Johns, "I want you to fly every man here to Straubing today in that C-47."

Johns had never flown a C-47 — hadn't even been in the cockpit. He made a beeline for the plane — found the flight engineer and said, "Say Buddy, close that door, and come up here and show me how to start this thing." He taxied to the end of the runway and took off — just the two of them. He landed at Straubing — took off from there and landed back at Kitzengen. The CO was waiting on him. "Where in the hell have you been? Didn't I tell you I wanted these people moved now?" "Yes sir — no problem," Johns said.

We began flying training missions immediately. Not far from Straubing there was an area where German tanks and trucks had been hauled in. Many of the pilots with lots of missions were deserting the squadron, that's how I actually felt at the time — they were deserting — but I was wrong. They probably should have been rotated out long before they were. Most of them had about 85 missions. Mayer, Johns, and Wilde had about 65. I had missed about 15 missions while I was grounded after getting shot down.

We were told that we had to practice dive bombing and strafing on the tanks and trucks. I thought, "What the hell." I'd had enough of this shit. Then I considered the possibility that they wanted the "now" older pilots to teach the younger pilots the ropes — and we did.

I was given a newly created job — recreation officer. Everyone was bitching and griping — including me — and I was ordered to improve morale and keep everyone happy. What an order. There was absolutely nothing to work with. We were out of whiskey. Doc was getting stingy with his medicinal alcohol, and there was no equipment for any kind of game — not even a checker board.

I was pointed toward Sgt. Gray. He was a real operator. Back in the states he had owned and run a midway in Tennessee. If there was anything to buy on the black market, he knew where it was.

He and I decided that the easiest and quickest way to improve morale was to find some whiskey. We went to operations and asked how long it would take to get some shipped in. "There won't be anymore," we were told. We'd have to pay and provide for ourselves. That was a hell of a note — all during the action we were plied daily with the stuff, and now they had cut it off — not only to us but the armored outfits and all — everybody.

The Sgt. said he knew where some scotch was, but that we'd have to go back to Belgium to get it — probably cost about $5.00 a fifth. I asked him if we'd buy it and bring it back and sell it or what? "No sir," he said. "We're going to take orders and collect the money before we go." I said, "OK, I'll work the officers and you the enlisted men."

After our canvass we laid our plans. We were going to be transporting lots of whiskey. Remembering Warren, I sent the Sgt. to the motor pool — told him to get a good jeep and enough jerry cans of gas to get us back — plus a trailer that had a cover to go over it.

The next morning we took off by daybreak. I took my flight charts to use as a road map. We made good time for a while, until we started hitting little towns. The streets were narrow and congested and slow to get through. We decided to make for the nearest autobahn. It was out of our way, but we had to be able to make better time. What a joy! We were zipping along, until we came to a blown bridge. The Germans had blown every bridge as they retreated. We would have to maneuver through fields — sometimes hills — and sometimes through villages to navigate our way to the other side of the blown bridge.

We took turns driving — about two hours a hitch. Late afternoon I said I was getting tired and that we needed to find a place to spend the night. The Sgt. said that if we could just hold out, he knew a good place not too far into Belgium. It was after dark, and I was driving. "We're getting close," he said. It was a typical cafe with rooms above. They fed us, and we went to bed.

The next morning we went on into Brussels. We had no orders. We were on our own. Sgt. had to make his contacts. We decided time and place to get back together.

I found and walked into an officers' mess for lunch. Then, I went sight-seeing. I even found the "piss boy" on this out-of-the way street — a little boy statue. He had gotten lost and when found was in that exact spot — peeing.

The Sgt. and I met. I said, "If you know where we can get some good food, I'll buy." When we arrived at the cafe, it was boarded up. I thought,

"Hell." The Sgt. said to follow him. He opened a door next to the cafe, and we climbed a flight of stairs to the second floor. He knocked on a door — the man looked us over — glanced down the stairs — and invited us in. We sat at a table for two. The Sgt. ordered for us. We had a drink — mine bourbon. Then soup — delicious, a salad with green stuff — the first I'd had in forever. The entree, with side dishes of vegetables, would you believe, and dessert. I was ecstatic. The bill was $22.00 for the two of us — in that day — a small fortune.

The next afternoon he dropped me off at the Schoofs, and said, "I'll be back early — about sun up — in the morning with the booze."

It was Johnny Walker Red Label scotch. The cases were stacked on top of one another. He had gotten a good buy.

While in Brussels, I had stopped by every office I could find with a Sgt. behind the desk — told them that we were stuck way down on the Danube — needed recreational equipment — and where could I find it. The answer was always, "Try Erlangen, Army Headquarters."

The base at Erlangen was just beautiful — large new brick buildings — houses for the generals and staff — scattered around — and landscaped to perfection. Our planners had made sure that not one bomb or bullet touched the place. That was going to be our headquarters.

I found the officer of the day's office — explained my predicament. He assigned me a Sgt. with keys — and we went down a long hall looking inside almost every room. He gave me part of what he had, which wasn't much — 2 bats, 4 baseballs and 2 gloves — checkers and chess — volley ball, no net — and a few other odds and ends.

Sgt. Gray and I had driven 496 miles the first day to Belgium. Our return trip was well over 500 miles. Sometimes I got to where I couldn't climb out of that jeep. I'd roll over and fall out on my hands and knees. We were pooped when we got back, but we made everybody happy.

Here came that damned Johns again with that poker faced smile — bless his heart. I had already flown to Kassel for him. "Now what," I said. "Well," he said, "One of our junior birdmen made two fishermen jump out of their boat on a lake at Munich. He bounced his P-47 off the water and was able to come down in a little airstrip at the edge of Munich." "And you want me to fly that plane back," I said. "The maintenance crew I sent down there to put on a new prop (the old one got bent back over the cowling) just called in to say they had it ready," he said.

I knew that Johns had to have someone that was capable, and that he could trust. Friendship — I loved him dearly — wasn't a factor. If the situation had been reversed, he knew I would ask him.

Another pilot piggy backed me in a 47 to the field. It was small. We debated whether he could get in. He made one pass with wheels and flaps down — judged his distance — came back around — barely cleared the fence — there was a 10 ft. high wood fence all the way around the field — dropped us in, and hit the brakes hard.

We taxied up by the other P-47. The ground crew was all smiles. The crew chief said that he couldn't get but 2400 RPMs out of the engine. 2700 RPM was normal for take-off. I walked around the plane. The bottom of the fuselage was bent up some. I climbed in — started the engine — and watched the instruments. Oil pressure OK — cylinder head temperature a little low — gas OK — rpm 2400 — I needed more. I shut the engine down — climbed out and told the crew chief to cut the tail wheel loose.

The other pilot said that getting that plane out of there would be risky. I had a plan. The field was round. I looked at the windsock and taxied around the fence until I was into the wind — turned my tail as close to the fence as I could — set the brakes — locked my tail wheel — and opened the engine until the plane was shuddering. My plan was to make the final decision when I was exactly half way across the field. At that point, if things didn't feel right, I'd pull the throttle — drop the rest of the flaps — open the cowl flaps — brake hard — unlock the tail wheel — and ground-loop before I reached the fence. The 47 would ground-loop at 60 mph, without dragging a wing.

I was past half way. The struts began to bounce. I held the plane on the ground and at the last minute lunged up and over the fence and over some trees and light wires across the street. After topping the trees I settled back down until my wheels got all the way up. I was blowing black smoke.

The ground crew had begged for a buzz job. My radio wouldn't receive and the other pilot could barely hear me transmit. I held up one finger and pointed down. We dropped — dived — into the field nearly to the ground on the opposite side from them and zoomed upright over their heads.

On the way home we skirted a huge thunderstorm. Lightning was flashing past us. I noticed something peculiar. There was a blue haze out on my wingtips.

My oil pressure began to drop a little. The engine wasn't running as smooth as I would like. As we neared the field, another storm was close to the runway. Planes were dropping to the runway like flies. I told the other pilot I had to get down and to start yelling "May Day," We greased our planes in, and just as I opened my canopy to taxi the storm hit.

I walked into operations and told them to take the plane out of service. It was unfit to fly.

A number of our pilots volunteered for a special project that lasted for days. I didn't. An army 6x6 truck would arrive early in the morning and take the pilots to a German airfield, or a factory, or a facility of some kind. They were to look for things that were different — that they couldn't identify. Then, after agreement with each other, crate the object up and have it shipped to the states.

Every day or so my flight would show up on the board. We'd go practice our bomb runs and strafing. The scuttlebutt was that we were heading for the Pacific and had to stay prepared.

Then, one morning, a hurry up move — we had to pack our things and get out. The engineers were going to put down a new runway. A new runway? What the hell was going on? Somebody must be screwy. It wasn't until 37 or 38 years later that I learned the truth. After the war Cotsie spent about 20 years in the OSS — the forerunners of the CIA. It was the Russians we were staying ready for. They were giving us trouble about the line where they were going to stop their advance.

We moved to Pocking, a little town further down the river — about five miles from the Austrian border. I packed my B4 and duffle bag to ship, but I folded my cot — bound it tight — and took it in the airplane with me. No way was I going to lose my dearest possession.

Pocking was in a farming area. The town was on a hill and most of the people lived there. One of our fellows borrowed an MP armband. He and a couple of others would go egg hunting. Fresh eggs were unheard of. All we ever got was powdered eggs. They would go to a house — knock on the door — and when someone appeared, he'd say, sounded like, "Habens zee eier?" The first answer was always, "Nein." He'd point to his armband and real mean like, repeat, "Habens zee eier?" The person would disappear and return with one egg — sometimes as many as three. When they got a dozen, they would quit for the day. No sharing.

They took the attitude that if you want fresh eggs, go out there and get your own.

After lunch one day, I went over to see Warren to ask him if he would like to take a ride in a piggyback 47. He was overjoyed. I had already taken my crew chief on a ride — no stunts — mostly straight and level, because that's what he wanted.

Warren and I got up and flew cross country awhile. Then I asked him if he wanted to do anything else. "Go to it," he said. I explained each maneuver — power off stall — power on stall. I'd ask each time if he were OK? — Sure didn't want to make him sick. Half snaps — half rolls — rolls. "Is that enough?" I asked. "Yeah," he answered.

Back near the field, I spotted a hay wagon pulled by two horses. It was late afternoon. About 20 people had loaded hay all day and were going home towards town. Six of them had climbed on top of the hay to ride. I said, "Say, Bud, you want to make those people jump off the top of that hay wagon?" "Yeah, Boy, " he hollered. I went to the other end of the field from the wagon — got lower and lower until the big 4 bladed prop was almost cutting more hay. Closer — closer — they were pointing — those on the ground began to run — four disappeared from the hay — the last two wanted to ride me out, but at the last minute — jumped.

Warren was ecstatic. I asked, "Do you want to see what time it is?" I had noticed a church spire on top of the hill. Across from it was the town hall with a clock in the tower. The street was narrow, so I went by the clock face with my wings vertical. We were within 6 or 8 ft. of the clock when we passed it.

On the ground Warren thanked me, "Bud, I sure do appreciate that." As he walked off, I noticed his legs were pretty wobbly.

Doc Milligan came up to me in the bar and said he was going to Heidelberg the next morning and did I want to go. I had suspected that he had been watching me pretty close since my crash. Martin, another pilot, I, Doc Milligan, and his sergeant left early the next morning in Doc's jeep.

The countryside was beautiful. At one point along a river we spotted a big white bird on the other side. We stopped — decided to target practice with the Sgt's. carbine — each shot twice — we could see our bullets hit the water — none close to the bird — it didn't even fly.

Near lunchtime we came to a small village. Some kind of an army unit was stationed there. Doc said,

"This is where we'll have lunch." He found the officers mess, and we were invited in.

Heidelberg was gorgeous — not a scratch on a building. The university was the town — classrooms, labs, etc. were in almost every building.

During the Seventh Army's advance, the commanding officer of an armored outfit sent a messenger under a white flag to tell the Germans that he wouldn't level the town, if they would pull out. They did, but they blew every bridge as they left.

It was getting late. Doc wanted to go to Stuttgart — might find some war booty there. It was after dark when we arrived — dreary looking place. We were in the French zone. Doc kept asking directions until we came to a large building. Doc told us to come on and for the Sgt. to be sure to bring the keys to the jeep. We climbed the steps and went through some large double doors into the foyer. At a desk a French soldier was all lolled back in his chair. What uniform he had on was dirty and smelly. He reeked of essence of grapes. His rifle was leaned against the wall. At Doc's urging, he shuffled off to another room where we could hear voices. What might have appeared as officer of the day teetered toward us. Doc explained that we wanted to get into the room with the war booty.

I felt uneasy. Those frogs could do us in, and nobody would ever know. We had no orders, and certainly no one would look for us in the French sector.

The Frenchman took us to a room and opened the door. He stayed outside; we walked in to a table that had nothing but junk on it. I eased up to Doc and whispered, "Let's get out of here."

I was tired. I slept most of the way back home.

Someone in administration, Cpt. Stith, I think, said that if enough of us wanted to go to "Eagles Nest," Hitler's hideout, that he would order a bus — G.I. Bus, of course.

Our first stop was Salzburg — Mozart — Mozart — Mozart — no wonder he was so creative. It was like a paradise — a special town unto itself. There was an ambience about the place that seemed to reach out and get you. The people seemed not to remember that a war was just over. I thought that maybe I'd come back someday and spend — maybe a month.

The Bavarian Alps made me think of my mountains at home. They didn't look the same, but it's the grandeur that all mountains have — a feeling of freedom — a feeling that you aren't so big — and when you're on top of one, a feeling that you are a conqueror of a sort. Oh! My mountains — my mountains. Home to my mountains. I'll get to see them again.

We passed through the little town of Berchtesgaden and on up the mountain. We could see the ruins before we got there. We climbed a path to what must have been something elegant.

Eagle's Nest

It was on the point of a mountain and had been bombed out — that is, from the first floor level up. From the first floor down was a concrete bunker that the bombs didn't dent. I walked through what had been the living room toward where plate glass windows had been. I stood there — and thought, *"I'm standing where a madman has stood. He was a human being, and I am a human being. What real difference was there between us? He was mad. Can I prove that I'm not?"*

Such thoughts! Oh well!

Herschel wrote on the back: "The boys taking in the view."

I walked through the window opening out on the terrace. The view was breathtaking. I gazed long enough to absorb some of the majesty into my being — turned and left.

The View Through Hitler's Picture Window

Our next stop was on the edge of town — a small two story hotel — about 40 rooms. The hotel had been built as a place for R&R for German generals. It was a brothel. Women from all over the world had plied their trade here — even some Americans.

Herman Goering had had a private passenger train in which he traveled all over Europe — and in the last days of the war ended up near here. It had been filled with the art treasures of Europe — paintings of all the masters — and lots more.

The furniture had been stripped from the rooms upstairs and all these paintings had been hung or leaned against the walls in each room.

MPs were everywhere. Each of us had to show our ID and sign a register when we entered the building.

I felt so inadequate — stupid in fact. I was looking at the greatest art collection in the history of the world and didn't have enough knowledge to appreciate what I was seeing. In one room there were five pictures leaning against the wall — the first one with its back turned out. I pulled it forward and looked — it was a Rembrandt — the other four were too. Good Gosh Almighty! I was handling — touching Rembrandts.

We were directed to a local cafe to eat. We had a floor show. There was a small stage at the rear. A troupe of German folk dancers began to perform. All the women wore long sleeves — long dresses that were highly colored and beautifully made. The front from neck to waist looked like a white bib.

The men wore frilly white shirts — short black leather jackets — short black leather britches — leggings — and high top shoes. They also wore hats — Tyrolean, I guess.

They danced ensemble — smaller groups — and some individually. The men would keep a rhythm going by slapping their hands — jacket — britches — leggings — and shoes. Fascinating.

We drank beer out of highly ornate steins. I remembered my great-grandmother Goodlake, who had come from Germany, had one.

While in Pocking, we lived in former German barracks. We paid some hunkies, we called them, to keep the place clean and make our beds. These Hungarians had been displaced by the Germans and used as slave labor. There were probably a couple of hundred of them. Every Saturday evening they too would put on shows — lots of talking — some singing — some dance — all rather boring. One couldn't expect to find much talent in a group like this, but I did enjoy watching how they entertained themselves.

All of us in our barracks were out playing volley ball one afternoon. All we had on was a pair of shorts. When we came back in the barracks, one pilot almost immediately reported that his money was gone from his wallet. We all made a dash. We had been cleaned out. The hunkies were accused. They became frantic. I guess they thought they would be shot before a firing squad.

In a few minutes their leader came waving his arms. An officer in uniform had been seen in the barracks while we were out — — — — — — — — — good description. It didn't take long to narrow the suspect down to one of our ground-pounders, who seemed to always be broke — gambled too much — and drank too much. He had gotten a 7-day pass to Paris. I felt sure the MPs arrested him when he got there. We never saw him again.

Now it was for sure. We were going to be sent to the Pacific. I went straight to Major Hardcastle and Capt. Stith and told them that I wasn't going — I had already done enough, and besides I had more than enough points to be returned to the states. Each person overseas, regardless of branch of service, was to be rotated when they got their points — so many for being in a combat theater — so many for meritorious citations — and so on. I think the number was 26. I had 31.

We left Pocking. I didn't even go pet my 47. I would fly another. We ended up in a staging area at Laon, France — north of Paris. We lived in tents again. We received our shipping orders — the numbers had to be stenciled in white paint on our bags. I hit Hardcastle and Stith again. "I'm not going. You can find someone else." "But, we've already put you in for Captain," they said. "I don't want to be a captain. I don't want anything to do with the Pacific. I've earned it, and I'm going to the states."

I went back and stenciled my bags. That afternoon we were told to paint the numbers out. More numbers — more paint out. This went on until I had white stripes almost around my duffle bag. Each day I would beard Hardcastle and Stith in their den.

The numbers stopped. We were told that everything had been put on hold. Hardcastle and Stith apparently wanted to get me out of their hair. Stith said that Mayer and I could have 7 days R&R in England, and that he would arrange transportation.

We got to London on Friday, because VJ [Victory in Japan Day] day was the next Tuesday, and the English started celebrating the end of the war in the Pacific on Friday evening before. There was pure bedlam. Thousands upon thousands of people were massed and mashed together in Piccadilly Square. Mayer and I backed up into a porch so that we could see over the top of the mob. We saw a phenomenon. While there was some milling about throughout the crowd — some holding hands — others hugging one another — some laughing — others crying — some couples turning round and round in place — small groups formed a ring around the people in the middle, starting on the right side of the mob was a mighty surge — like a spearhead. It moved to the left. There was nowhere for it to go because of all the people — but it went — getting faster and faster — almost to a run — gathering more and more people in its wake. There seemed to be only one person in the lead — at the rear it was at least 50 people across from side to side — all picking up speed. As the salient headed toward us on the left, it veered towards the middle of the mob — and then — all at once, it just dissipated — like nothing had ever happened.

How people in front of that movement kept from getting trampled is still a mystery to me today. During the evening there were other movements in the crowd, but nothing like the first one. Mobs unnerve me. One person has no defense. A mob seems to have a will of its own.

On Tuesday afternoon Mayer and I got off the train in Edinburgh. The train ride had soothed my soul.

The smoke from the steam engine furling back — the clickity clicks of the rails — the sound of the brake rigging clasping the wheels — hearing the steam whistle when someone opened the door to the vestibule. I was transported.

Then came the lowlands — the heaths of Scotland. I gazed out the window — some were close — others farther away. I imagined seeing people of long ago gathering their bundles of faggots — wearing their dreary clothes — moving ever so slowly. Their eyes were blazing — piercing into mine.

I saw the reflection of Uncle Gus's face, in the glass of the window — my great grandfather. He had on his felt hat — his white beard glistened against the dark sky, and his eyes, those penetrating eyes, were looking all the way through me. I had been here before. I had lived on the heaths. Something inside me told me I had. Things felt familiar. One day — maybe I'll go home to the heaths — again.

In Edinburgh I was awed by the beauty of the castle — steep rock cliffs all around except for a steep walk from the town to the main gate. The castle appeared to perch up in space, and particularly, that night with the spot and flood lights shining up to the castle. We were told that was the first time the lights had been turned on since the beginning of the war.

It was V-J Day. The laddies and lassies were dancing. Across the main street from our hotel was a park, and down at the foot of a hill was a pavilion. Most of the people in town must have been there and most just watching the dances — which were called by name or number — something like our square dancing. Most of the dances were very physical. One dance started out like a round dance, but, at a certain cue, the couple that was in a certain corner of the floor would hold hands and gallop diagonally across to the opposite corner — 70 to 80 feet away. The gallop was sideways and very fast — each couple in their turn trying to outdo the ones before. Some people got knocked down — some couples fell — but each time everyone would let out a yell — including Mayer and me.

Fascinating. We came back after our dinner and watched until bedtime. Happy, joyous people that had spent years of wartime, and now they were celebrating the end of it all — and for us too. Happiness is contagious. We were sharing with them. Tears came to my eyes. I was so thankful that they, that Mayer, and that I had made it through the guts of hell.

We had flown over to England, but we had to take a boat back. It was a boat, not a ship. We arrived at a port, south of London, after dark — at the appointed time. We were told that we couldn't sail until the tide came in. We were shown some bunks down in the hold near the prow. We took off our jackets and shoes and stretched out — and, soon, both of us were sound asleep.

When I awoke, we were moving. I slipped into my shoes and climbed the steep steps to the deck. We were bobbing around like a cork. I went to the rail and stared at the horizon — trying to keep my sense of balance. Someone down the rail started upchucking over the side. The wind was blowing. That did it. I wheeled — grabbed a 5 quart bucket hanging on the wall — bounced down the steep stairs. I was seasick — damn it to hell. Mayer was too. He had his butt stuck out the door of a little cubical and was using the toilet. After retching several times I lay on my back on the bunk and stared up at the ceiling — and thought, "Mayer and I can't win. Everywhere we go we get sick and start up-chucking."

The English Channel lived up to its reputation. It was rougher than a cob.

Days and weeks passed in the staging area at Laon. I felt worse than hell — no pep — no nothing. It seemed I had to struggle to get to the mess tent. I figured I was going through a let-down of some sort. Having operated at my utter capacity in combat, I now was just lollygagging around — spending too much time in the sack.

All we were doing was waiting, waiting to get orders to ship out home. Glory Be! Jumping Jehosephat! We were moving out to Marseille — all the way from northern France to southern France to get a ship home. My fretting was over. I didn't care what I had to do; all I wanted was to get on a ship.

Southern France — at least that time — was a lot like a desert — dry — dusty. Looked like it was worn out. In a large deep ravine just north of the camp, a stage — theatrical stage — had been built for the US0 performers. Lots of big names did their act there. The ravine made an almost perfect amphitheater. One night Mayer and I walked up to the rim. Thousands of GIs were sitting on the ravine floor. Thousands more were perched — where possible — on the walls — and thousands more on the rim. I now knew what a multitude was. The sounds coming from a multitude were different from anything I had ever heard — the applause — the yelling — echoed back and forth through the ravine. The spontaneous responses from a multitude take on different dimensions from a crowd. There are no individual voices. There is only one voice — that of the multitude — a voice of eager happiness.

Mayer and I watched very little of the show. We were too enchanted with the fireflies — the lighting of cigarettes on the opposite rim — some on the canyon walls — in the distance on the canyon floor. They twinkled — one — and then several — sometimes whole pods. They made patterns — some that we could even anticipate.

As I lit my own cigarette, it gave me a warm feeling — I twinkled back at all those men now assembled in peace.

The ship had docked. That word sent a shiver of elation through me. The waiting was over — so I thought. One day went by — then two — three. I began to have unnerving thoughts — am I going to get on board? Maybe they've miscounted? Will they allow standing room only?

Back in our tent area, a sergeant came by and said that we should report to the loading dock. Joy! Joy! Joy! There was still a long line boarding the ship — step by step — pick up our bags — move one step forward and put them down. We were next to the last unit — only officers. Our enlisted men were already on board. The last unit was a bunch of nurses.

Now, I understood what had taken so long. Each man or nurse had to be stowed away somewhere — some said 6,000 — some said 8,000. All I knew was that that babydoll was loaded to the gills.

Then, one of those unbelievable, uncanny events that happen in war time happened. H. L. Moody — Harry — had been on the ship for three days and was watching the loading process from a deck away above us. He recognized me. He told me later that he started jumping up and down and yelling to the soldiers around him, "I know that boy! I know that boy! That one. The tall one. We grew up together back home."

H. L. and I had gone to school together — played together — hunted — and rode his pony together. H. L. lived on a farm that fronted on Springside Road. I lived on Long Shoals Road, and one of the Moody fields almost reached to our property. He always had lots of chores to do — getting wood into the house — plowing out a crop — and hoeing the weeds out.

One late summer afternoon H. L. and I were inspecting their watermelon patch — a beauty, it was. Some of the melons would run 30 lbs. or more. I started testing them for ripeness by thumping them with my middle finger. H. L.'s mother was just above us and called to me to stop that thumping — I would make hard places in them. I was ashamed and explained that I didn't know any better.

Another day later on that summer H. L. said to come and see how to make molasses. They had grown a big patch of sugar cane, and when it was ripe, Mr. Moody got a neighbor to move his molasses mill to the patch. First the cane was cut and hauled to one side of the press. The press was two metal rollers that were turned by a shaft about six feet high. On top of the shaft was mounted a log pole — a sapling — with the butt end overhanging the shaft to nearly balance the long end. The long end was linked to a horse that went round and round and round — turning the rollers. One person fed the cane — piece by piece — between the rollers. The juice would squirt out and flow into a vat. Another person tailed the squeezed cane out of the rollers and carried arm loads to a stack outside of the horses' rounds.

Then came the evaporating table — made out of sheet metal — turned up about 1" all around — with dividers that didn't go all the way to the other side. The hottest fire — wood — was the first section where the raw juice was poured in. The juice would bubble and steam. When it got the right color of brown — it was moved with wooden pushers with a handle about like a broom handle to the next section — and to the next. Molasses making is an art. If the juice ends up with a greenish tinge, it's got a biting taste and will spoil in the jars. If it gets overdone, it'll have a burnt taste and turn to sugar in the jars.

Anyway, H. L. and I started peeling sections of cane and chewing the pulp to get the juice out. Best stuff you ever tasted. I couldn't or didn't stop. After I went to bed, I started dreaming I had to find a place to pee — there were all those people around the mill — I finally spotted a big oak tree. I peed in my bed. I woke up almost immediately. I was the most embarrassed 12 year old boy in the whole world.

I didn't know that H. L. had seen me until the train ride from Camp Kilmer, N. J., to Fort Bragg, N.C. A Lieutenant came into our car. "Is there a Herschel D. Ponder in here?" He asked. I raised my hand. "Do you know Harry Moody?" I thought long and hard. "No, I don't believe I do," I said. "He says he knows you, Harry L. Moody," he questioned. I said, "You mean H. L.? Good damn almighty. Yes."

Lord, it was like he was from another world. I hadn't seen anyone in service from home since before Miami Beach.

We set sail. I was free of the land of chaos — that almost cost me my life — a land where most people had endured great suffering and misery. Someday I might like to visit Europe again, but it wouldn't be anytime soon.

The next day came with a thick, heavy, overcast. Word was passed along that we would see Gibraltar on our right before too long. Its shape was more like a mirage, but we could figure out the shape. I crossed to the other side of the ship. There in the distance was a stretch of dark, ominous, foreboding land. Africa was known as the Dark Continent in those days. It agreed with the glimpse I got. I never had any desire to visit such a land — and still don't.

Three or four nights later I drew a watch — the navy called it a watch — the army — guard duty. 12:00 midnight till 4:00 a.m. My station was the deck below the bridge deck at the first crossthrough from the front. As instructed, I had my life preserver on. Absolutely no one was to be in this area at night with the exception of the ship's crew. I watched the deck on one side — would cross through the passageway — and watch the deck on the other side of the ship. The wind began to pick up. It blew harder — and harder — and harder. It was steady — no gushes. I had to go to the leeward side (Uncle Gus would say winard or lurard). The deck was slanted to the right, and it stayed there — no rocking back and forth. The ship was quartering — knifing into the wind, which was so strong that it had us laid over about 20 degrees. I thought, "Steady as you go, mate. Don't let her get broadsided. We'll blow over."

All kinds of objects were blowing off the ship. Anything that wasn't securely lashed down was gone. All kinds of stuff zipped by me so fast that I couldn't recognize what it was. I began to think about, if I were asked, what I would report. I couldn't identify anything. Maybe I'd just say, "We sure had a big blow."

The next day was clear and sunny. The sea was a gigantic fury of waves — cresting way up in the air — the white spray streaking and glistening in the sunlight.

The nose of the ship would rise to great heights — hang with a moment of suspension — and then plunge out of sight into the sea. Under — under — under — and then "Thar she blows" — bursting forth with a mighty spray into the winds. The seawater would run the deck to the sides and disappear. Majestic, she was — a thrill to see her work — to work for the seafaring men, who must have loved her much.

New York harbor — a sight that had stirred the insides of millions of people coming from lands far away. There she was — that fair lady — holding her torch up in the sky for me. "Yes, dear friend, it is I, and I am home." She blurred from the tears in my eyes.

Some nice lady with a wonderful smile handed me a coke as I entered the doorway of the building fronting the dock — another, a bar of candy. I thought "that sure was a nice gesture." I ate my snack on the bus to Camp Kilmer.

On the train to Ft. Bragg, as I was returning to the seat from seeing H. L., a sergeant touched me on the arm. "Lt., I was on the homing station the day you got shot down. I was trying to do what Warren said to do, but I had a problem in figuring out who was hit. Then, I realized it was you. The problem was that when Cotsie transmitted, his voice was high pitched, loud, and rather frantic. Your voice was slow and matter of fact as if nothing had happened."

I thanked him. He asked, "You really had a close call, didn't you?" "By all the odds possible, I'm not supposed to be here," I answered.

OCTOBER 29, 1945 –

FORT BRAGG, NORTH CAROLINA

I got my discharge papers.

I was free. Free from being used — used by people who considered me a pawn in their plan of destruction — free from being a number. "Ponder, Herschel D. — 14133614 — or — 0-715588, officer number. "

I had to — did consider that I should stay in service. I was an emotional and a physical disaster. They caused it. Let them take care of me — or would they? The larger question was — could I make it in civilian life? At age 23 I had lived a complete lifetime. From the time I was a boy, I went to school, studied, learned, graduated, trained, and received an advanced degree — a DPD — Damned Pilot of Destruction. I was a professional, one with extensive experience. Should I resign from my profession, this regimented way of life?

If I resigned, did I have enough left in me to start a new life — start all over again? I didn't know. At

Ponder Anew What the Almighty Can Do

that moment I felt that I had been used — used up — I was utterly drained — and I felt that somebody — somewhere — owed me something — didn't know what — but something.

The easy way out seemed to be to try to stay in service — but I didn't!

It was in the afternoon when I got my discharge in hand. I had already studied the bus schedules. I found a telephone and called my daddy at work — we didn't have a phone at home — gave him the route and time I was supposed to arrive in Asheville — that is, if the bus wasn't over full and I couldn't get on it. He said, "We'll meet you down the road somewhere." The bus trip took 10 to 12 hours back then.

Mom and Dad figured Statesville was as far as they should go — to be sure they didn't miss me. They had looked at the passengers on each bus from Raleigh. When my bus pulled in, they were standing on the platform. We three with our arms around one another — hugged one another — kissed each other — cried — and hugged some more.

As we topped Old Fort Mountain, there was the faintest hint of dawn in the east. I had come from the east — over water — by train — by bus. We

258

had just climbed the crooked road from Old Fort —
out of the lowlands — and were passing through
Swannanoa Gap into paradise — my beloved
mountains — which I would never leave again.

Mom said that we'd have breakfast before going to
bed. She said, "Looks like I have to put some meat
on those bones." My Dad used one of Uncle Gus'
favorite expressions, "You look like a grubworm
with the shit slung out of it. What did they do to
you?" When I enlisted, I weighed 160 pounds —
now, I was in the lower 120s. I was 60 years old
before I got back to 160 again — but it wasn't from
the lack of good food.

I would never forget the breakfast we had that
morning — sausage, bacon, eggs, grits, toast, and
Mom's delicious homemade strawberry jam — and
hot tea with milk and sugar in it. It was a moment
and a lifetime since I had eaten her good cooking
before.

After I got up Dad told me about Wimpy, my dog,
"Bud, he couldn't make it until you got home,"
tears filling his eyes, "But he made it till May 8
[Victory in Europe Day], until he knew you were
safe."

Wimp was a big dog — part collie and part
German Police — and smart, my goodness sakes

alive. He had a lot more sense than I did — out-figured me all the time. I never did get the best of him.

Dad said, "We buried him up behind the shed. Come on, we'll show you." Mom said, "We found him under his favorite bush there by the back porch. He was so heavy that your Daddy like to have never got him loaded in the wheelbarrow."

Behind the shed my Dad had dug a hole. He lined it with tarpaper, and Mom had found some old lace curtains in the pack room that they put on top of the tar paper. My Mom helped Dad get Wimp down in the grave — put more curtains and tar paper — said a prayer for him and filled the hole. Dad found a big rock for the headstone.

Duck hunting season opened on November 2nd that year. Dad said that Slim Estes and Smokey Ballenger were coming by about daylight to pick me up.

They had scouted the river and had plenty of high powered prewar shotgun shells saved, my Dad said, till I got home. We put in at Penrose. That was the farthest up the river that we had ever put in. They knew where the ducks were. All the other hunters would have put their boats in on down the river where it was Bridge — Glen's Bridge — Longshoals — or Shut-in at Sandy Bottoms.

We had floating the river down to a science. It took two cars — we'd leave one where we were going to take out and pull the boat with the other to where we put in. Where we left the first car depended on how full the river was — the amount of rain that had fallen. Before the war and with the river at bankfull stage, we'd float from Horseshoe to the sand drag at Carriers Field — a small airport in the edge of Asheville. From Shut-in on down was through the Biltmore estate. They owned the property on both sides of the river. Their rangers would threaten to arrest us. If they caught us on the river one more time, they'd pull us in. We'd say, "Yessir" and pay them no mind. By law the river was a navigable stream, and they couldn't keep us out.

Smokey's boat was a 14'0" metal, almost flat bottomed. It had a pointed nose and three seats. Slim and I sat on the middle seat side by side — mainly so we could talk. Smokey paddled the boat, we floated as close to the bank as we could and would take the inside on big bends. That day the ducks were scattered perfectly down the river. We flushed them out from behind drifts and tree trunks in gangs of 4-6 and 8s. My Daddy's Mod. 12, full choke, Winchester pump gun held seven shots, and had a kick, with those high powered shells, like a mule. I shot that gun so many times that up in the day I began to flinch every time I pulled the trigger.

Slim and I were talking — 4 ducks came up. We went bang bang bang bang — and never touched a feather. Smokey got on us. "You fellers pay attention up there." Around the next curve 4 more came up. I knocked three to the water with my first three shots — missed my fourth and got the fourth on my fifth shot. Slim was firing an automatic and was pulling the trigger before he got lined up on the duck. Smokey said, "That's a shade better — four up and four down."

The boat seat was only about 10" from the floor. We had to keep at least one foot back under the seat to balance the recoil of the gun. My legs were cramping — stretched my left foot straight out to rest my leg — big gang came up — bang bang — my fourth shot drove me off the seat. I ended up on my back with my head between Smokey's knees. "That's all right, Herschel, that's all right. I know another feller that gun did the same way." My Daddy. I had let my right foot get too far from under the seat.

I had seen some of my kinfolks, but what I really wanted was to see Eleanor. She was at Chapel Hill in a short term switching from quarter to semester system. The next day after duck hunting I went to the Western Union and sent her a telegram — been duck hunting STOP see you in two days.

It was almost dark when I got to Chapel Hill. I started hunting Carr Dorm. Navy men had lived there during the war and had just moved out. I walked into the lobby and saw a girl at a desk. I told her that Eleanor was expecting me. She sent a runner.

The lobby was full of young men and women — giggling and laughing. I was the only one in uniform. I was ill at ease. My uniforms were the only decent clothes that I had. I waited. I wondered if she would recognize me. I had lost a lot of weight. I waited. I was kinda ashamed of the way I looked. I waited. The waiting wasn't really very long, but it seemed forever to me.

She came down those steps. I felt my face flush. My God — she was beautiful — even more than I had remembered. Her smile glowed. All the giggling and laughing seemed to stop. There was an aura around her. In that moment I knew she was my life. I don't want to be a detriment to her, but whatever the future would be — please, Good Lord, let her share her future with me.

I touched her — I held her hands. We looked into each other's eyes. I kissed her — and then — we held one another.

We got engaged on Christmas Eve. Sometime after dark it began snowing — soft, big wet flakes. I made it to her house by using the road that crossed Enka Lake Dam. I visited with Eleanor and her family for a good hour. When we went out to get in the car, the snow was nearly up to the hub caps. Her father said that I'd never get her back home without chains. "I've got a set in the trunk," I said. Her three-years-younger brother, Jim, volunteered to put them on. When he was on his back under the car fastening the inside link, he was mumbling — I thought I heard, "I'll tell you one thing, she ain't worth it."

We made it to midnight service at All Souls in Biltmore. What a wonderful church! What a wonderful place! I was truly home now — and so proud to have Eleanor beside me. I knelt — and thanked the Good Lord for my survival — asked his forgiveness for committing murder — and asked his blessings on Eleanor and me.

I was so humble, for I truly felt His presence. Later in the spring Eleanor and I were in the Episcopal church in Chapel Hill one Sunday morning, and as the preacher started saying, "The grace of our Lord Jesus Christ, and the Love of God, etc.," a movement caught my eye. I saw the Lord walk down from the chancel, across to, and through the east wall into a courtyard. Until now, I never told anyone except Eleanor. Through the years there have been other incidents, but that was the most dramatic.

I was beginning to realize that combat had done two things to me. It had dulled my mind — my body — my feelings. It was like I was trying to look through a shield that was around me. And yet — it had left me incredibly sensitive — sensitive to the moments — my moments — of other people's involvement with one another — their love for one another, or kindness — the sharing of joy or grief between them — the perfection of their artistry.

Many times my moments are filled with tears that I can't keep back. Sometimes the hair will stand up on my arms with a goose pimple at the base of each. I can feel my scalp tingle — my insides quiver — and there's a lump in my stomach.

Children always do me in. I used to take my pre-school daughters to my Mom's first grade Christmas party. She made sure that each child — including mine — had a present. I knew that for some of her pupils that would be the only present they'd get for Christmas. I couldn't stand it. Using all my will power not to, I'd still cry. I'd make it to the cloak room or dash outside the door. Men are not supposed to cry.

The first time I saw Eleanor cry bothered me a whole lot. We were talking about people — what to expect from them. She said that people were filled with goodness to their core and that's ultimately what would come out. I said that she was going to be disappointed a lot of times and not to expect anything out of anybody — and if their goodness did come out — great joy was to be had. I said, "Eleanor, people will lie, cheat, and rob you. They'll use you — they'll even kill you." That did it. It didn't help when I added, "I put my trust in the Lord — not people."

Her philosophy has worked for her, and I guess mine has for me.

I have believed that if one man mistreats another, he has sinned against God. I have lived all through the years with my back to the wall — intending that no man ever use me again.

I registered for the spring semester while visiting Eleanor in November. In January I lived in Stacy Dorm and Eleanor moved to Kenan. We usually had supper together in Lenoir Hall — a cafeteria. Occasionally, we'd splurge and eat at the Port Hole — and maybe take in a movie. I was in a dream world. The shock of the sudden change was quite difficult for me. Only a few months before I was flying in combat — and now — in this beautiful place of peace — where people seemed to play all the time — where I was madly in love — where there never seemed to have been a war — I was working like hell to keep my insides from jumping through my skin.

I have told many people that if it hadn't been for "Blue Heaven" and Eleanor, I very probably wouldn't have made it. Bless her heart.

Dr. Das Kelly Barnett was the preacher at the Baptist Church. He heard that Eleanor and I were engaged. He sent for us. He didn't ask us if. He told us what we were going to do — Eleanor would attend six meetings in his office and I three — the first and last together. He advised Eleanor to see a gynecologist. His counseling to both of us was invaluable. At our last meeting he said, "Whatever town or city that you pick to live in, visit a number of churches before you decide which church you'll join. Join the one in which you'll feel most at home and do the most good in the Lord's work." A Baptist minister saying that? I nearly fell through the floor.

He was a man — a man ahead of his time. He had written several books about social justice — and for his stand — the Southern Baptist Convention black-balled him. We wondered what happened to him. Several years later I saw a one-inch article in a railroad trade paper that Dr. Das Kelly Barnett, Episcopalian minister, was to speak before the Texas legislature urging a 50 cents an hour minimum wage for the wetbacks from Mexico. He was a man that practiced what he preached. I have always felt honored that I knew such a man.

I went to see the manager of Victory Village — a barracks (one story) type complex that the Navy had used — and now would be used for married couples in school. I was told that he couldn't even put me on the waiting list until we were actually married.

We found a bedroom in the home of John and Myrtle Hinson — no cooking privileges and had to share the bath with the family — for $45 a month. Married couples housing was almost non-existent.

We were married on June 22, 1946. We spent our honeymoon at Nags Head. Rookie Lee and her new husband, Tommy, had invited us to share a cottage — owned by Rookie's parents — with them for one month. We lasted three weeks. There were very few cottages and practically nothing else on the island. Our one big night out we drove down to Manteo and saw "The Lost Colony," — beautiful show.

In September we returned to school. At the first opportunity I went to see the manager of Victory Village, and he put our names on the waiting list. Boy! We were we way down. About a month later I checked by again. Some names had been marked through, but we were still too far down. Another month — still the same. I was getting $90.00 a month under the G.I. bill. Our room was $45.00. That left $45.00 to eat on and pay tuition and fees for us both. No way baby! Before Christmas break I went to the manager again — explained income and bank account — and told him he was going to be personally responsible for two people not graduating from Carolina. Finally, he said that he had an opening for summer school. I was overjoyed. I shook his hand and thanked him — and told him we would stay out of school the spring semester — and see him in June.

It was about 4:00 p.m. the day we headed home for Christmas break. We had loaded the trunk of our 35 Ford coupe with things we could spare until the end of the semester. Will A. Shuford, Jr. was riding with us.

We headed toward Pittsboro, where we could get on U.S. 64. We were barely out of Chapel Hill when I saw a Navy Hellcat skimming the tops of the trees under a heavy overcast. I nudged Eleanor and said, "Wonder what that damn thing is doing around here?"

At Pittsboro we turned right onto 64, and up ahead all the cars in the right lane were stopped. My first thought was that a plane had crashed (which it had) and all those dodos wanted to see it. The first and second cars in front of me pulled into the oncoming lane — other cars followed us. We were moving great until we got to the top of a little hill at the edge of town. A State Trooper stopped us.

We sat there awhile with the motor running — the battery in the coupe was down. I said, "Will A. we might as well go take a look." There were a number of people looking down the bank of the right shoulder. I told Eleanor to keep her foot on the gas pedal just enough until the needle was on the charge side. There were houses on our left with front yards that had a sloping bank to the road. Will A. and I walked up the bank and about 300 ft. past the first car. All at once a Hellcat — with wheels and flaps down came in low over our car. I thought, "Well, he wants to get a good look at his buddy that had crashed, and that's as slow as he can go." He wobbled on down the road and I noticed he made a flat turn and nearly hit some oak trees on the hill in the distance. He was now headed toward us. I thought, "Well, he wants to take another look at his buddy." I saw his glide break. The son-of-a-bitch was landing straight into us. All the alarms went off. I ran the top of the bank toward Eleanor — screaming and motioning for her to get out of the car. She did — stumbled on the bank to her knees — and I glanced back. The plane was veering toward the bank — the propeller was eating Will A. up. — Turned out he fell down the bank and wasn't touched. All I could see was the dark under the running board of the coupe. I yelled to Eleanor to go back. She stood up. I was getting close. I dived off the bank to tackle her and get us down. The left wing of the plane hit us both. He had left about 4 ft. of his left wing in the front car. Part of the jagged edge had hit me.

I was on my back when I could see. Two men had Eleanor standing up. Just as I got to my feet, the pilot of the plane came running up. He was a naval lieutenant and had a brass name tag on — J. R. Mackay, Jr. Somehow I learned he was from California. I wanted to insult him the best I could. He started off with, "I'm sorry. I - - - - I' I cut him off, "You damned stupid do-do. What are you, a student? Or a damned junior birdman?" His eyes fell and he took a step back.

All at once I saw another Hellcat in the distance headed toward us — wheels and flaps down. We were trapped. I had to get us to a safe place. I spotted a rock wall beside a filling station across the road that would be better than nothing. I managed Eleanor through two cars in our lane. Somehow, I got Eleanor over the tongue of a trailer in the inside lane — and to the rock wall. Eleanor began having trouble standing up. I propped her against the wall. Will A. ran to us. Then this voice from above us — a lady standing in her yard — said, "Would you like to bring her into my house?" I looked up into her face. I flushed. I knew she was an angel. Maybe she didn't — but I did.

Will A. and I made a pack saddle with our hands and arms — got Eleanor's arms around our necks — carried her around the corner to the walk — up the steps onto the porch and through the front door. We put her feet on the floor but kept her arms around our necks. She said, "Look." There was a picture on a table beside the sofa. "I know that boy. I went to Mars Hill with him. It's Marion Petty." Mrs. Petty said, "That's my son."

We sat Eleanor down on a bed in a room that was also used as a sitting room — got her coat off — and some of her clothes. She had the shakes bad — by now. I covered her up and asked Mrs. Petty for another blanket. She brought the blanket and then a hot bowl of home-made soup. I thought, "It looks a little greasy — but it's hot." I said that I had to find a doctor. After about the fourth spoon of soup, Eleanor got sick at her stomach — Mrs. Petty ran for a pan — and I repeated, "Doctor."

Dr. Camp had his office in his home. Said he'd be there in a minute. He examined Eleanor and gave her a pill. Eleanor kept begging to go on home for Christmas. He bandaged my arm and left.

Eleanor got over the shakes, but she couldn't move without her back hurting. I went for the doctor again. It had been about two hours since he had seen her before. He felt and pressed her lower back on the right hand side. He said, "If she doesn't go home tonight, she's going to be so sore in the morning that she can't move — maybe several days." Eleanor begged. He taped her from the middle of her stomach — around and past her spine — from the top of her buttocks up about 14" to 16" — gave her a small capsule for pain — handed me three more and said, "If she comes to before you get to Asheville, give her another one."

I told Will A. to sit in the middle and to lean hard against Eleanor so she couldn't move.

Every time we started slowing down she would start moaning — and as sure as we stopped — she'd upchuck. I'd tell Will A. to hold onto her —

I'd jump out my side — run around the car — jerk her door open — and we'd hold her over the running board until she got through. When we'd get moving again, I'd drive that 35 Ford as fast as it would run. I gave her another pain pill — yellow jackets the Doc had called them.

I dropped Will A. off at his folks' driveway — and thanked him. At my folks' home I got Eleanor's right arm around my neck and hoisted her out of the car. On the back porch I managed to get hold of a scrub pan hanging on the trellis wall, because I knew what was going to happen — and it did.

The next morning she couldn't bat her eyelids without hurting. I went to Skyland about daylight and called Dr. Herbert — sweet and kind and rough as hell — all at the same time — former Navy — and could cuss worse than Satan himself. We didn't have a phone at my house. I also called Eleanor's mother.

Bessie got there first with Doc Herbert right behind her. He took one look at Eleanor and started cussing Dr. Camp. "There's no way that stupid bastard could tell if her spine was hurt by just feeling. We're going to the hospital and get X-rays. I'll send the ambulance and meet you at Biltmore Hospital — damned stupid bastard."

I held the screen door for the two men with the ambulance as they rolled Eleanor out on to the porch. Snow had been falling for a very short time and the ground was already covered — great big flakes — some as big as silver dollars — silently falling so thick that our voices were muted. A shiver ran through me. The snow was an omen — an omen that Eleanor would be all right. Both were so beautiful. I lowered my head, and from within my heart, said, "Thanks."

As the two men started down the steps with the stretcher, they hesitated while one of them pulled a towel over Eleanor's face. All at once Bessie let out the awfullest wail one ever heard — startled the hell out of me.

All the X-rays were OK.

One day a newspaper photographer came by and took our picture — made the paper with appropriate story — hell-uv-a-way to get your picture in the paper.

I got to take Eleanor home on Christmas Eve. In the meantime I had been working up a claim against the U.S. Navy — put down the exact cost of everything I could remember — hospital — doctors — drugs — laundry — replacement value of torn or damaged clothes. I was sure I hadn't remembered everything. I was plumb sick over my flying jacket — it had been torn and ruined. There wasn't enough money to replace how I felt about it. And a Clemson shirt that I was wearing — the impact of the wing on my back had caused several slits in the front of the shirt.

One year later — the next December — the Navy reply was that they would pay half of the claim. Damn the Navy! Damn Navy pilots — damn the eager beaver Navy bastard that cut the claim in half.

I called Dr. Herbert — should I sign the release? Would Eleanor have any lasting effects? Could she get pregnant? He said that I might as well sign.

I called a lawyer. Henry Fisher said, "You'll have one hell of a time getting anything out of the U.S. government. Sign. "

I signed. The total claim had been about $500. I accepted the $250. We were all but broke.

All of this had been caused by six Navy pilots flying Hellcats that took off from somewhere in Penn. to land in Greensboro. They got lost in a snow storm in Virginia and were running low on fuel. One of the six had sense enough to go to the

Raleigh Durham airport and land. The others —
well — — — — — — —

I have always suspected that the State Trooper that
was responsible for clearing three miles of highway
for the others to land on had, sometime or other,
been in the Navy.

What a hoot! — fly 51 combat missions — get shot
down — and come home and get hit on a public
highway by a damned airplane — a Navy airplane!

After exams for that semester we went home for
the whole spring semester. While there I went to
see Dr. Herbert several times. Through a bunch of
tests — and his guess was that I had under active
thyroid gland. He said he didn't exactly believe it
because I was supposed to be fat and heavy — not
a shadow like I was. It wasn't until 1949 with
Doctor Armentrout, Internist, that I got regulated
to the right maintenance dosage — 4 grains a day.
Today, I'm down to 1-.2 Synthroid and 1-1 gr.,
thyroid a day.

In the meantime I was having a hell of a time in
school. My mind would go blank — that is —
blanker than usual. Other days I would do very
well. Dr. Armentrout said that it was like my
thyroid glands had a physical injury — like part of
them had been cut out with a knife.

We returned to Chapel Collitch [College] in June — in a heat wave that neither of us will ever forget. Both of us got down on our hands and knees — me in a pair of shorts and Eleanor in shorts and halter — and scrubbed the wooden floor of our new home in Victory Village. Sweat literally dripped off our chins. Every now and then I would have to get a drink of water — so I could get behind Eleanor and watch her action.

That was our first home together. A two burner electric hotplate that wouldn't boil water around 6:00 p.m. each day — and a refrigerator that was kept cool with blocks of ice — ten pounds every 2 or 3 days. We were so happy.

Eleanor Israel Ponder and Herschell Ponder

Vetville, U.N.C., Chapel Hill, N.C.

We made a Claude Thornhill concert in Memorial Hall — a couple of big dances — and watched Charlie Justice play football. He was truly a triple threat — a magnificent person and athlete — and friend.

Our two room apartment cost $22.00 a month plus $2.00 for extra furniture. We were going to make it. While in service I sent an allotment home each month, and with my mustering out pay had saved $3,000. With that I bought the 35 Ford coupe, got married, paid all our bills in school, and with the $90 G.I. bill lived on the rest. At the end of our last semester, fall of ' 47, we were flat broke. No money has ever been better spent.

On our way home for Christmas break that semester, Eleanor and I decided that this was as good a time as any to begin our procreation process, but nothing happened. I was concerned about Eleanor — the lick from the airplane, but we decided that my virility would be checked first. I went to Doctor Herbert. He opened the door where I was waiting and motioned for me. I followed. He said, "Look in that microscope." I never saw so many squirmy things. I lifted my head and looked up. He said, "Son, you're pure dynamite. Better keep that thing in your britches."

One day I went out to the A&H Flying Service at the old airport off Mills Gap Road. All of the local fellows were real cordial to me — shook my hand — and welcomed me as a fellow pilot. They encouraged me to get my civilian license. After all of the exams, I qualified as a "commercial-single engine" pilot.

Several friends said that they would love to take a ride with me. Slim Estes asked if I would teach him to fly. We had two lessons. I wondered why he quit, but then I realized I was probably too rough on him — yelled at him a couple of times and banged his knees with the stick. That's the way I was taught and thought that was the way it was to be done.

Henry Fisher, whose brother was an Eastern airline pilot, said that Eastern was hiring single engine pilots that were 6'0" and over. I was a natural — a shoe-in. I would fly co-pilot for 18 months and then get my own run. It sounded like one chance in a lifetime — good pay — an easy life.

Henry's brother sent me an Eastern application that was several pages long. I got about half way through filling out the forms and stopped. I was about to break a vow that I had made in Zwartberg when I saw the flak map of the Ruhr Valley — "If I lived through all that flak facing me, I was going home and stay home even if I had to dig ditches to stay there." And, I've dug a few.

I tore the application up. I was through flying — my flying career was over. My friends had had the rides they wanted. Slim had quit his lessons. That was it. I reasoned that I was like a soldier that carried a rifle. He brought the rifle home and put it in the closet. I would now put my 8-50s and 500 pounders in the closet.

In fact, I didn't get into another plane until the fall of 1959. Manly Wright took 22 of us to the Carolina-Michigan football game at Ann Arbor in the Northwestern bank plane — a converted C-46. Carolina won only two ball games that year, and one of them was Michigan at Ann Arbor. What a game. Whoopee!

Soon after I began to write this epistle, I began to realize that the shield around me was gone — that I have had a freedom of expression that was only possible before the war. I have loved it; I feel as though a load has been lifted off me.

So, my three girls — today, three beautiful women — you are a part of my new life that began with Eleanor. What love — what joy I have had with her and you.

october 29, 1945 – Ft. Bragg, North Carolina

Your mother and I have not wasted a single day since we met. Every one of them, in its way, has been a jewel.

To you three I say, "Don't let something so precious slip by — think, plan, work, enjoy, love, be happy, and most of all: "Ponder anew, what the Almighty can do."

YOUR DAD

About Carol Ponder and Robert Kiefer

Carol is Herschel Ponder's middle daughter and is married to Robert, her partner in all things. In addition to preparing Herschel's memoir to share with the public, they also have created a two-person reader's theater play telling her father's story. They have crafted a performance of words from the memoir, family stories, and songs of the period (both popular and traditional). It is a beautiful production that evokes the essence of war and warriors, their victories, sacrifices, loyalty to each other, and the sweet pain of coming home. The audience response from combat veterans and other people from many walks of life has been tremendous. In the post-performance talkbacks, people of all ages share stories they may never have told before.

This is their mission for the production, entitled *Ponder Anew: A WWII Warrior's Story*:

We hope that sharing Lt. Herschel D. Ponder's story from the stage will act as a catalyst for healing and reintegration for veterans of all ages in the context of their families and communities. We honor their service and hope to raise awareness in all audiences about the seen and unseen wounds endured by those who serve in our Armed Forces in any generation.

Carol and Robert have been theatre and music professionals since the 1970s. Taken together, they have acted, sung, and danced in thousands of performances and hundreds of productions. Carol is an award-winning singer of Americana with a specialty in *a cappella* balladry and, like her father, is a consummate storyteller. Since 1987, she has worked as an award-winning teaching artist, consultant, and project facilitator in education through the arts. She plays guitar, autoharp, and spoons and has appeared on the Kennedy Center Millennium Stage as well as at dozens of arts centers, schools, and clubs in the United States and in Northern Ireland. Robert is a theatre director, as well as actor, with a specialty in developing one-person shows, whose work has been seen at the Piccolo Spoleto Festival in Charleston, in colleges and universities, and in arts centers around the country. His most recent work, *Harriet Beecher Stowe: A Literary Soldier,* was performed at Bowdoin College as part of the celebration of Harriet's 200th birthday. He has directed everything from Shakespeare to musicals to Beckett. Robert also directs and produces Carol's music, concerts, and recordings and worked for 20 years in the art department on feature films, music videos, and commercial work. Seasoned professionals in all aspects of theatre, Carol and Robert are delighted to be working together to create and perform such a powerful and valuable work of art.

For more information and to book performances of *Ponder Anew: A WWII Warrior's Story*, go to :

http://carolandrobert.com or

https://www.facebook.com/PonderAnewAWWII WarriorsStory